No one on the planet knows more about procrastination than Fuschia Sirois—her groundbreaking research has transformed how we understand its roots and remedies. In this e̶n̶g̶a̶g̶i̶n̶g̶ ̶b̶o̶o̶k̶ e of the science and offers practical insig s off. Postpone reading it at your own r

—**ADAM GRANT, PHD,** #1 *NEW YOR* F
THINK AGAIN AND HOST OF THE TED PODCAST *WORKLIFE*

A superb book written by a scholar with more than 2 decades of groundbreaking research helping us understand how procrastination undermines our well-being and health. Dr. Sirois provides clear explanations about the many factors that contribute to our procrastination combined with practical exercises to facilitate change. This is a book that can help you end self-defeating delay in your life.

—**TIMOTHY A. PYCHYL, PHD,** ASSOCIATE PROFESSOR,
CARLETON UNIVERSITY, OTTAWA, ON, CANADA, AND AUTHOR OF
SOLVING THE PROCRASTINATION PUZZLE: A CONCISE GUIDE TO
STRATEGIES FOR CHANGE

I have seen too many people who have had their lives ruined by procrastination. Fuschia Sirois has provided a valuable book that reflects her unparalleled understanding of what causes procrastination and what needs to be done to address it. The practical suggestions and exercises found in this book will restore the hope of procrastinators who decided long ago that they would never be able to escape their tendency to make life more difficult. People who are desperate for help will certainly benefit from this book.

—**GORDON L. FLETT, PHD,** PROFESSOR OF PSYCHOLOGY,
YORK UNIVERSITY, TORONTO, ON, CANADA

This book is a valuable companion to individuals struggling with procrastination. Fuschia Sirois provides insights into the unique psychological processes of procrastination. Self-compassion and self-forgiveness are presented as two innovative starting points to overcoming procrastination.

—**PROF. DR. CAROLA GRUNSCHEL,** PROFESSOR OF EDUCATIONAL PSYCHOLOGY, UNIVERSITY OF MÜNSTER, GERMANY

Now is the time to revisit the science and solutions of procrastination. In this readable and friendly book, Dr. Sirois updates and expands information on the causes, consequences, and "curse" of procrastination based on psychological science. It's a good read, for those who want to end procrastination now.

—**JOSEPH R. FERRARI, PHD,** ST. VINCENT DEPAUL DISTINGUISHED PROFESSOR OF PSYCHOLOGY, DEPAUL UNIVERSITY, CHICAGO, IL, AND AUTHOR OF *STILL PROCRASTINATING? THE NO-REGRETS GUIDE TO GETTING IT DONE*

Procrastination

Procrastination

What It Is, Why It's a Problem,
and What You Can Do About It

FUSCHIA M. SIROIS, PHD

AMERICAN PSYCHOLOGICAL ASSOCIATION

Published by
APA LifeTools
750 First Street, NE
Washington, DC 20002
https://www.apa.org

Order Department
https://www.apa.org/pubs/books
order@apa.org

In the U.K., Europe, Africa, and the Middle East, copies may be ordered from Eurospan
https://www.eurospanbookstore.com/apa
info@eurospangroup.com

Typeset in Sabon by Circle Graphics, Inc., Reisterstown, MD

Printer: Gasch Printing, Odenton, MD
Cover Designer: Mark Karis

Library of Congress Cataloging-in-Publication Data

Names: Sirois, Fuschia M., author.
Title: Procrastination : what it is, why it's a problem, and what you can do about it / Fuschia M. Sirois.
Description: Washington, DC : American Psychological Association, [2022] | Includes bibliographical references and index.
Identifiers: LCCN 2021059060 (print) | LCCN 2021059061 (ebook) | ISBN 9781433838064 (paperback) | ISBN 9781433840340 (ebook)
Subjects: LCSH: Procrastination.
Classification: LCC BF637.P76 S57 2022 (print) | LCC BF637.P76 (ebook) | DDC 179/.8--dc23/eng/20211217
LC record available at https://lccn.loc.gov/2021059060
LC ebook record available at https://lccn.loc.gov/2021059061

https://doi.org/10.1037/0000302-000

Printed in the United States of America

10 9 8 7 6 5 4 3 2

CONTENTS

ACKNOWLEDGMENTS

This book would not have been possible without the collective wisdom on procrastination uncovered by counselors and scholars in the field, such as Burka and Yuan, who through their experienced lens of counseling psychology aptly noted the important role of emotions in procrastination years before the scientific research community got on board with this idea.

I'm also eternally grateful for the support, inspiration, and encouragement of my long-time mentor (and friend) Tim Pychyl, who was the first to introduce me to this intriguing field. It was his curiosity and compassion for the phenomenon of procrastination that inspired me to steer my research toward the complex and troubling waters of understanding procrastination.

Lastly, this book would not have been possible had it not been for the encouragement, humor, and support of my husband, Mike. Whether as a sounding board for ideas, offering help and feedback on the illustrations, or just to hear me rant when I was struggling with the writing, without him I would probably be someone wanting to read a book like this rather than being the one writing it.

Procrastination

INTRODUCTION

I don't see how he can ever finish, if he doesn't begin.
— Lewis Carroll, *Alice's Adventures in Wonderland*

Do you know someone who procrastinates? For many of us, the answer to that question involves taking a quick, and maybe guilty, look in the mirror and an uncomfortable "yes." But don't despair: You are not alone. Procrastination is unfortunately something that most of us are familiar with. We've either experienced it firsthand or observed it in others. And it's something we want to stop. We would rather feel energized and productive when we make progress on a project or proud when a coworker or family member accomplishes what they set out to do. That is where this book can help.

If procrastination is more than just an occasional lapse for you or someone you know in your personal or professional life, then this book is for you. As you will discover while reading this book, procrastination can have negative and often serious effects across many different areas of life. The consequences of procrastination—which can range from work performance and productivity, to academic life, personal relationships, finances, and even physical and mental health—are far from trivial, especially when procrastination has become routine. So, if you are someone who manages employees, assigns academic work, counsels people on their finances, provides support and guidance on physical or mental health, or simply wants to be more understanding of and compassionate toward the people you know who procrastinate, then this book is also for you.

You may be wondering why you should trust what I have to say about procrastination; after all, there are numerous books and blogs written by people about how to deal with procrastination. Few, though, have the 20+ years of experience researching procrastination that I do. I have published more than 30 scientific research articles and book chapters on the causes and consequences of procrastination, and I have delivered more than 100 talks on procrastination to scientific organizations and the public. So you can say that I am an expert on procrastination, professionally. But procrastination also holds personal significance for me. I've witnessed the toll procrastination has taken on family members and even myself. In writing this book, I've realized that I am more of a procrastinator than I care to admit. The irony of sometimes procrastinating while writing a book on procrastination is not lost on me. It is these personal observations and struggles, along with my professional expertise, that are the source of the unique insights, guidance, and tools I provide in this book.

A DAY IN THE LIFE OF A PROCRASTINATOR

Procrastination usually involves a particular task that needs to be done, often by a certain date that was set by ourselves or someone else. Or, as with writing a will or getting a mammogram, the task has no set due date but still needs to be completed. In either case, for reasons that are not always clear at the outset, we just can't seem to bring ourselves to do it. Whether the task is big or small, when we procrastinate and put off a particular task we know there will be unpleasant consequences for not having taken timely action. Sometimes it may not be obvious that you are procrastinating until it's too late. Consider, for example, the following scenario, which may have a ring of familiarity:

Yet another day has passed, and Pat finds himself struggling to sit down and get to work on his task. It's that same task he has attempted to complete for 3 days in a row but with no success. It's that same task that he knows he has to get done today, or he will be letting people down and breaking promises that will cost them (and him) money. It's that same task that has made it hard for him to fall asleep at night because he is worried about whether he can do a good enough job on it. Today, when he sits down, he notices his chair isn't quite comfortable, so Pat convinces himself that a more comfortable chair is what he needs to finally get this task done. While going to retrieve the comfy chair from the other room, he notices a pile of papers sitting in disarray that needs to be tidied and organized, so he spends a few minutes organizing and filing. Feeling proud of himself for doing this, and mistaking busy-ness for productivity, Pat decides to treat himself with a well-deserved break on social media. Two hours later, he realizes that he is now hungry and it's lunchtime, so he decides it's best not to start that task until he's eaten. After all, he'll have better ideas, think more clearly, and have flashes of inspiration when he has a full stomach and no distracting stomach gurgling.

After lunch, however, Pat only feels sluggish and sleepy and even less motivated because there is now only half a day to work on a task that he reckons will take the whole day to complete. He reasons that it's best to wait to start until tomorrow now and get a fresh start after going to bed early and getting a good night's sleep. But as Pat is trying to fall asleep he is flooded with feelings of guilt, shame, and regret for not making progress with that task today. His thoughts turn to an unhelpful chorus of "Why couldn't I just get started?" and "What's wrong with me?" that further amplifies how bad he feels. He realizes that it's again going to be difficult to sleep—he needs a distraction. So he decides to go on his smartphone and view mindless TikTok or YouTube videos as a distraction to chase away those negative feelings so that he can finally sleep. Two hours and more videos than he can remember later, Pat is no closer to falling asleep or to feeling less ashamed of his lack of productivity and broken promises. It's now well past the time he wanted to fall asleep, and his hope of being well rested so that he can be productive tomorrow is quickly fading. And so ends another day of procrastination, with unfulfilled responsibilities, lingering shame and guilt, and yet another night of broken and restless sleep.

This anecdote highlights some of the immediate and more obvious costs of procrastination: lack of productivity; potential financial costs; and feelings of guilt, shame, and regret. As you will learn in this book, though, these aren't the only costs. Procrastination, if left unchecked, can erode trust in your professional and personal relationships, take a toll on your physical and mental health, and rob you of reaching your goals and achieving your full potential in life.

WHAT YOU'LL LEARN FROM THIS BOOK

It's tempting to entertain the idea that simply bringing the consequences of procrastination to light might be enough to halt it in its tracks. I, for one, would be overjoyed if this were the case. Sadly, though, like knowing that engaging in unhealthy lifestyle habits will most certainly lead to poor health later on, simply knowing the full range of impacts from procrastinating is not enough to end this problematic behavior. Awareness is important, yes, but if you want to find sustainable solutions for reducing procrastination, more is needed. This is why it is so important to understand the deeper reasons why we procrastinate.

By the end of this book, you will be able to

- recognize the psychological processes that lead to procrastination,
- develop effective ways to manage your automatic responses to the tasks on which you most often procrastinate,

- make changes to your environment so you're less likely to procrastinate,
- build skills to manage the situations that can trigger procrastination,
- become more aware of the internal scripts that can maintain procrastination,
- recognize when perfectionism may be feeding procrastination, and
- learn new ways to view tasks to reduce procrastination.

I hope that you'll also feel

- less ashamed about your procrastination,
- accepting of the uncomfortable negative emotions that may drive you to procrastinate,
- motivated to take action on your unfinished and lingering tasks, and
- compassionate toward yourself when you struggle with procrastination.

TO BE HUMAN IS TO PROCRASTINATE

Procrastination is a rather unique human behavior. On the one hand, we can recognize and accept that putting things off is a common problem for many people. This makes procrastination an easy target for jokes, jests, and puns. If you're like most people, including myself, you've procrastinated at some point in time, and this may be one of your motivations for reading this book. In fact, you may have seen the title of this book and said jokingly to yourself, "Sure, I'll read this, later." If so, you might imagine me bantering back, "Congratulations on making it to the Introduction!" It is exactly this commonplace nature of procrastination that makes it easy to dismiss it with light-heartedness and sarcasm.

On the other hand, however, for many people procrastination is anything but a laughing matter. Pat's scenario is a good example of this. Anyone who occasionally procrastinates, including myself, might joke about procrastination on the outside while at the same time secretly knowing that we should be getting on with that task. Few people are proud of their procrastination and, if they are, then it probably isn't true procrastination (I discuss this further in Chapter 1). For others, procrastination can be a far more serious matter. Habitual procrastination may have robbed them of their dreams, their sense of self-worth, and their health and well-being. It may have had lasting and damaging effects on their relationships with their coworkers, supervisors, partners, family members, and friends.

We also tend to hold unflattering beliefs about people who procrastinate. When you think of someone who procrastinates, what traits come to your mind first? Maybe you think of someone who is lazy or impulsive. Or perhaps you think of someone who lacks discipline, has difficulty managing their time, or is unreliable. These are common responses when I ask people what they think of people who procrastinate. As I discuss in Chapter 4, there are good reasons why procrastination is associated with some less-than-desirable characteristics.

The problem is that when you are the person who has procrastinated, these same negative characteristics and judgments come to mind. We feel bad, and often ashamed, when we procrastinate. It's in these moments that we can easily forget that procrastination is something that almost everyone has done at some point. The realization that procrastination is so common doesn't make it something that should be ignored or left to creep back again; instead, acknowledging procrastination as being common and widespread can pave the way toward us accepting, understanding, and resolving it so that we can reach our goals and fulfill our potential.

When we minimize or laugh about procrastination, we may be trying to cover it up or manage the not-so-obvious feelings of guilt, shame, and self-blame we have about this uniquely human weakness. What we need instead are insights, strategies, and tools to help break the inertia of old habits and replace our default reactions to unpleasant tasks with ones that motivate us to take action. This book aims to provide you just such a toolkit so that you can better calibrate your efforts to reduce procrastination and choose the best strategies to effectively match your own situation.

FOCUS ON CAUSES, NOT SYMPTOMS

If you've looked into how to deal with procrastination before, you've probably come across a variety of different approaches and advice. The news and popular media, as well as self-help blogs and gurus, promote a host of strategies: manage your time better, put an end to your laziness, strengthen your willpower, become more motivated. Although some of these tactics have merit, they don't always address the complexity of issues that are central to understanding and managing procrastination.

Each of these strategies/approaches tells a different story about procrastination and its causes that can be more or less complete. Some of them offer explanations for certain aspects of procrastination, such as why adding structure to your tasks can make them more manageable. Others might emphasize the value of reducing distractions to rein in impulsivity. From where I sit, though, these common approaches to dealing with procrastination only highlight the symptoms of procrastination, for example, difficulty getting started with tasks that seem large and overwhelming and letting temptations and distraction derail our best intentions. This isn't the same as answering the bigger question of *why* people procrastinate. In short, these popular approaches often lack a more in-depth view and understanding of the underlying psychological processes that can characterize and explain most instances of procrastination.

The focus of this book is on understanding and addressing the causes, not just the symptoms, of procrastination. You can always take temporary, Band-Aid steps to address the apparent symptoms of procrastination, but these will be less effective and less likely to result in sustainable habits than will addressing the core reasons why you procrastinate. For example, if someone is in pain, you can certainly make them more comfortable and give them pain medication, but if you don't directly deal with the pain's source it will likely continue or even become worse. I use this analogy not to medicalize procrastination but because it's one that seems most fitting to convey this point. We can think of procrastination in a similar way: Until you address the root causes of your procrastination, it is likely to continue to be an issue even after you have implemented other strategies that might seem reasonable.

THROUGH THE LOOKING GLASS

In this book, we'll explore the underlying reasons why people procrastinate through the looking glass of mood regulation. From this perspective you'll learn about how issues with managing mood, not time, lie at the core of procrastination. This is a view of procrastination and how to address it that is not commonly known and may seem opposite to what you might expect. Some of the ideas about procrastination that I present in these chapters can be counterintuitive and, at times, thought provoking, but all of the ideas, strategies, and approaches we explore in this book are informed by evidence and theory, two ingredients that are essential parts of any scientific approach that endeavors to better understand human behavior.

I also believe it's important that any discussion of procrastination should include the voices of those who struggle with this common form of unnecessary delay. In one research study, I asked people to write about a time that they had procrastinated and to share, in as much or as little detail as they liked, what had happened and what they had experienced. One of the things I learned from this is that people are all too willing to share their personal experiences of procrastination, especially if their responses are anonymous. But I was also taken aback by how much detail they shared about their experiences and by the extent to which many reported struggling with their emotions when they procrastinated and suffered as a result of their procrastination. Examples of these experiences are featured throughout the book to illustrate key points and takeaway messages. If any of these excerpts resonate with your own experiences, then all the better. Remembering that procrastination is an experience that many of us struggle with is an important theme that runs throughout the chapters of this book and one that underscores many of the approaches for reducing procrastination that we will explore.

What I'm also hoping you'll learn from reading this book is that there is no formula to stop procrastination, no one simple rule to follow if you want to reduce your procrastination for good, especially if it has become an unwanted habit. This is mainly because the apparently rational reasons why we procrastinate are in fact quite complex. They exist within a system of our beliefs, personality traits, habits, past experiences and memories, physical and social environments, hopes and fears and, most important, emotions. In a human system, formulas that attempt to explain procrastination will only scratch the surface of the dynamics involved. Taking a formulaic approach overlooks the complexity of these dynamics and the power of the various factors and forces that can drive and maintain our tendencies to unnecessarily put things off. This approach also overlooks procrastination as a very real human problem that deserves to be dealt with compassionately.

The insights and approaches that I offer in this book are instead based on accepting and even embracing these complex and often irrational forces that can drive our procrastination. When we see procrastination as being mainly an issue of difficulty in coping with negative emotions, then it becomes clear that if we want to reduce procrastination we need to understand and reduce the sources of these emotions. Why we might see a task as being unpleasant, or why we may feel stressed from thinking about doing even the simplest of tasks, can vary across people, tasks, and circumstances. This book will give you the insights and the tools you need to understand and address the reasons for the negative emotions that fuel procrastination.

Of course, there are some common sources and reasons why a task may cause us to feel frustrated, uncertain, anxious, stressed, fearful, or just plain bored and make us want to procrastinate. We'll explore what these are and how they can be dealt with using science-informed solutions throughout the book. But whether we actually do procrastinate that unpleasant task is often decided by how aware we are of our emotional reactions to that task and by the tools we have for managing the sources of these emotions. Thankfully, awareness and management of the negative states we experience when faced with a task can be learned and acquired and are the focus of several chapters in this book.

OVERVIEW OF THE BOOK

Having a set of concrete, ready-to-implement tools to tackle procrastination is crucial for reducing procrastination and any urges you may have to delay unnecessarily. I could easily provide you with this toolkit in just a couple of brief chapters, but I'd like to leave you with something more by the time you finish this book. I'd like to empower you with new insights and strategies to better understand and reduce procrastination in a sustainable way. After reading this book, you will have a broader understanding of procrastination and its consequences as well as a better understanding of the sources of the negative emotions that can drive procrastination. You'll also learn different ways to manage these negative emotions, whether they are acute jolts of stress, frustration, or anxiety or more lingering feelings of shame and guilt from procrastinating.

To meet these goals, this book is structured into three parts. The chapters in Part I (Chapters 1–4) deal with understanding and recognizing what is and is not procrastination. Now, you may be thinking that this should be obvious—who doesn't know what procrastination is? As we will discuss in Chapter 1, though, procrastination isn't as easy to spot as most people think it is. In Part I we will also review how and why procrastination can have harmful consequences across a number of important areas of life. The intent is not to be judgmental or to stir up feelings of shame for procrastinating—anyone who has procrastinated will know that we do this quite well without any outside help. Instead, we review these consequences with the aim of becoming more accountable for our procrastination. Plus, on the flip side, you'll develop a better understanding of the gains and improvements you can experience in different areas of your life when you use the strategies and tools described in this book to address your procrastination.

In Part II (Chapters 5 and 6), we will deep dive into the underlying reasons why we procrastinate, from the perspective of short-term mood regulation. All behaviors have an origin story. Procrastination's origin story is rooted in the negative emotions we experience when faced with certain tasks. We'll explore the psychological science that explains why mood matters when it comes to understanding and reducing procrastination and the unexpected relationships between mood and our perceptions of time. We'll also examine the "why" of the negative emotions we can experience when we are tempted to procrastinate and the thought habits and beliefs that often fuel and even amplify any negative mood we can have in relation to the tasks we may be struggling with.

The third and final part of the book (Chapters 7–10) pulls together all the evidence-informed insights from the previous chapters to present and explain a set of strategies and tools to help reduce procrastination. We cover a range of approaches that are known to be effective for helping people dial down negative emotions and resist falling into the trap of short-term mood regulation. It's equally important, though, to replace old habits with new ones that can fuel motivation to stay on track with your tasks and goals. We'll explore strategies that can help achieve this and examine some of the usual suspects that can contribute to procrastination, such as distractions and social temptations, and discuss why and how to best deal with these procrastination triggers from the perspective of mood regulation.

In every chapter I have included short "Take a Moment" sections and longer, end-of-chapter exercises to help you to begin to apply what you have learned. These will also provide you with an opportunity to test-run some of the tools and strategies featured in the chapters. My 20+ years of research and teaching have taught me that people learn best through active engagement. Having firsthand experiences with new concepts and principles through these activities can deepen your understanding of what they are and thus deciding whether they are right for you. Some of these activities are based closely on the research discussed, and others are ones I've designed specifically for this book. Although I hope these activities will be helpful, it ultimately will be up to you to decide which will work best for you on your own journey toward understanding and reducing procrastination.

Reading this book and engaging with the exercises will take you on a journey toward a deeper understanding of what procrastination is and of the reasons why you procrastinate. These insights can empower you to change how you view your tasks, your goals, and yourself. The repertoire of strategies, insights, and tools for reducing your procrastination are based on an alternative view of procrastination that places your emotions at the forefront. According to this view, responding to your procrastination in a kinder and gentler way is not only something you deserve but actually one of the best ways to ensure that you can and will complete your tasks and goals on time and with compassion toward yourself.

I

HOW PROCRASTINATION AFFECTS YOUR LIFE

CHAPTER 1

PROCRASTINATION: AN ALL-TOO-COMMON PROBLEM

You may delay, but time will not.

—Benjamin Franklin

In this chapter, you'll learn

- how to tell the difference between true procrastination and simply delaying something that you are supposed to do,
- how to assess your own tendency to procrastinate,
- why true procrastination can't be a "good" thing, and
- why you procrastinate and how your mood and emotions are involved.

Procrastination is a pernicious and all-too-prevalent problem in modern life. Whether you have been delaying writing that report that you know will be closely scrutinized by your boss, haven't quite gotten around to reorganizing the guest room for the visit from the in-laws, or have been putting off that call to a friend to apologize for something said in anger, chances are at some point you have procrastinated on a task that you know you should be doing. The good news is that you are not alone. If you are like most people, including myself, you've procrastinated at least a couple of times in your life, if not more, on something that you know you should have done right away. Or you may have succumbed to procrastinating on your goals and tasks rather frequently, and unnecessary delay has become an ongoing, habitual issue. Whether you procrastinate occasionally or more frequently, it's probably something that you don't feel good about doing.

Researchers estimate that 15% to 25% of adults habitually procrastinate (e.g., Steel, 2007). For example, people engage in procrastination frequently and across a variety of different tasks and a number of areas of life, including work and career, finances, education, romance, personal goals, and even health. Although these estimates may suggest that procrastination isn't really all that much of an issue, consider these points. First off, we are talking about one in four to five people who procrastinate on a fairly regular basis—not occasionally, or once in awhile, but very frequently. They regularly put off doing things they should be doing to meet their work, personal, financial, and health goals. As I outline in Chapters 2 through 4, the costs of procrastination can accumulate over time and take a toll on well-being across a number of important areas of life.

Procrastination becomes more of a concern when we consider a particular population for which procrastination is rampant, namely, college and university students. For this group, the numbers are both shocking and somewhat expected. Estimates from research on the frequency of procrastination among undergraduate and graduate students suggest that anywhere from 80% to 95% have engaged in procrastination at some point during their academic life (Steel, 2007). This means that at some point they have, for example, put off studying for tests and exams, delayed doing homework, or completed assignments and term papers at the last minute. Given the time demands of academic life, it's not hard to imagine why so many students find themselves procrastinating their academic work at least once. The high rates of procrastination among college and university students are also why they are one of the most heavily researched groups in examinations of this topic.

Unfortunately, for some students, putting off their academic work occasionally becomes more habitual. Researchers have estimated that approximately 50% of college and university students engage in procrastination on a regular basis, and this becomes their modus operandi for dealing with challenging or unpleasant academic tasks (Steel, 2007). Although procrastinating once in a while may be expected to have only a minimal impact on academic achievement, research has confirmed that, for students, doing so on a regular basis, and perhaps across a number of academic domains, can be very detrimental to academic performance.

When procrastination becomes frequent and more than just an occasional behavior, researchers refer to this as *chronic* or *trait* procrastination. It reflects an enduring personal characteristic that is like a personality trait. Now, this does not mean that a tendency to procrastinate can't be changed; quite the contrary: Personality traits, including procrastination, are not necessarily bred in the bone or hard wired into someone's personality. Think of trait or habitual procrastination as being an enduring tendency, or what personality researchers often refer to as a *characteristic way of behaving*. This may still sound like your behavior defines who you are and that you are at the mercy of your habits. To some extent this is true if you let your habits run their course without intervening. But we always have the option of becoming more aware of our behaviors and taking the steps needed to change them.

WHAT IS PROCRASTINATION?

Up to this point we have been discussing procrastination as a behavior that can happen occasionally or frequently, only in specific areas of life, or across a number of different domains or types of tasks. But we haven't actually discussed what constitutes procrastination, apart from it being a type of delay. Before we delve into the psychological science of when and why people procrastinate, the consequences of procrastination, and what we can do to reduce procrastination, it's important to have a good understanding of exactly what does and does not constitute procrastination. To accomplish this, we need a clear and precise definition so that we can be sure that what we are observing in ourselves or others is indeed procrastination and not some other garden variety form of delay.

As a psychological scientist, it's critical that I use a good technical definition of *procrastination* when I conduct my research. This is important because I must know that the data generated from my research are valid and that the conclusions that I draw from these data about the causes and consequences of procrastination are meaningful and relevant. If I want to better understand the psychological processes that underlie procrastination rather than those involved in making simple delays or some other related behavior, having a good working definition is essential; otherwise, it will be difficult to develop and test possible ways of reducing procrastination. This is also true for your own attempts to find ways to manage procrastination. If what you think is procrastination isn't actually procrastination but some other form of delay, the techniques and strategies that I discuss in this book are not as likely to be effective.

Whether viewed as an occasional behavior or as a more chronic tendency, most researchers define procrastination in roughly the same way. The definition below is one of the most widely recognized and complete definitions of procrastination researchers use:

> Procrastination is a common self-regulation problem involving the unnecessary and voluntary delay in the start or completion of important intended tasks despite the recognition that this delay may have negative consequences.

Although this definition necessarily has the word "delay" in it, you'll also note that a number of other key elements qualify the particular type of delay procrastination reflects. When we deconstruct this definition you will begin to see what makes procrastination both unique as a human behavior and so problematic.

Unpacking Procrastination

The first part of our definition classifies procrastination as a *common self-regulation problem*. We've already discussed just how common procrastination is, so this is not surprising. Viewing procrastination as a self-regulation problem is in many ways central to understanding both what procrastination is and the processes that underlie it. Self-regulation involves the processes that people use to manage their thoughts, emotions, and behaviors. In practice, this involves three sets of related activities: (a) setting goals, for example, making an intention to write a 10-page report; (b) engaging in the actions needed to accomplish the goal, such as starting to write; and (c) monitoring your progress toward reaching the goal, such as checking how many pages you have left to write, so that the goal can be reached.

With procrastination, the process of self-regulation can be broken down in terms of taking action steps; this is why we say procrastination involves a delay in the start or completion of an intended task. In other words, if an intention were not made to complete a particular task or reach a goal, then there can be no procrastination, so, for example, if you did not set a goal to write a 10-page report, and didn't write one, then we can't say that you procrastinated. Although this may sound fairly obvious, it is a critical and defining aspect of procrastination that can make it more difficult for people to spot in the real world.

The next key component of our working definition of procrastination is that it involves both *unnecessary* and *voluntary* delay. If we unpack these terms, it becomes clear how other forms of delay might be mistaken for procrastination. Using our previous example, if you had intended to write a 10-page report by Friday and a family medical emergency arose that meant that you had to pause all work-related tasks, then technically you are not actually procrastinating if you fail to complete the report by Friday. Your delay under these circumstances is necessary and to be expected.

For delay to be true procrastination, our definition suggests that it also has to be voluntary. In other words, delaying the 10-page report would be something that you chose to do. If, for example, your boss told you to put aside finishing the report by Friday because there was an urgent request from a client that you needed to deal with, then this would not be procrastination. You didn't choose to put off writing the report; your delay was a result of a direct order from your boss to do so and is therefore not voluntary.

The final component of our definition of procrastination is one that is often forgotten or overlooked and can lead to people confusing regular delay for true procrastination. In addition to each of the components we already discussed—the delay is unnecessary and voluntary, the task was intended—the delay needs to occur *despite the recognition that this delay may have negative consequences*. This final part of our definition of procrastination is also linked to one part of the definition you may have thought that I had overlooked: the idea that the task has to be an important one. In fact, I was saving that key element until now. It only makes sense that if you put off an important task things likely will not go well. We may not always know exactly how badly things will turn out if we procrastinate, but on some level there is a recognition that it would have been better all around if we had not delayed that task.

It's also important to consider what we mean by *negative consequences* when we define procrastination. Although these consequences might not be entirely clear at the point at which we decide to procrastinate (notice I referred to this as a *decision*, underscoring the idea that procrastination involves a choice to delay), there are usually some likely negative outcomes for oneself and others when we procrastinate. These can include fines and penalties when, for example, reports or tax returns are submitted late. The negative consequences from procrastinating can also take less tangible forms that are equally damaging. For example, much of the research I have conducted over the past 20 years has clearly shown that procrastination is linked to higher stress and, in turn, poor physical and mental health outcomes. In Chapters 2, 3, and 4, I focus on these consequences in more detail.

Procrastination can also negatively affect others, such as when it takes place at work or when it involves the delay of a personal task that has repercussions for friends or family members. Going back to our example, handing in that 10-page report late may damage your company's reputation or mean that a business opportunity is forfeited. But emerging evidence demonstrates that procrastination can negatively affect the reputation of the procrastinator in the eyes of others. I discuss this more fully in Chapter 4.

In short, regardless of the particular negative consequences that may result from procrastinating, or whether you know exactly how those consequences might take shape in advance, procrastination involves a recognition that this unnecessary delay will have a negative impact. It is this recognition of the potential negative impact that makes procrastination distinct, and potentially more damaging, than your run-of-the-mill delay. A good example of this is the immediate and negative impact procrastinating can have on your mood. People who procrastinate don't feel joy or pride when they put things off. Numerous studies have shown that, instead, people who procrastinate can feel a range of negative emotions, from guilt and shame to anxiety and self-loathing (e.g., Flett et al., 1995). We delve more into how and why negative emotions are implicated in procrastination starting in Chapter 5.

More Than Just Delay

You'll have noticed that up to this point I have been making reference to procrastination as a form of delay. But I've also been careful to point out, repeatedly, that it should not be confused with a garden-variety delay. To do so means that you could make yourself feel worse about a delay than you should. Alternatively, by mistaking procrastination for simple delay you may convince yourself that you are not actually procrastinating when in fact you are.

Delay can take myriad forms, from one that is due to *reprioritizing*—as in the example above, when your boss asked you to prioritize the upcoming client visit over the report—to *involuntary delay*, to *sagacious delay*. Falling ill and being unable to start or complete a task is an example of involuntary delay.

Sagacious delay, also called *wise delay*, also is not procrastination. This form of delay involves making a decision to temporarily put off an important task rather than pushing ahead with it because you are lacking key information, support, or other resources that are essential to successfully complete the task. For example, let's say that you've been asked to write a report about your company's online advertising activity over the past month, but you have been given the details for only the last 2 weeks. Because you don't actually have all the information you need to write the report, you can't complete it. In this situation you would need to contact someone and request the missing information so you can write the report. In these circumstances, delaying the writing of the report is a wise decision that will enable you to write a quality one.

How Do We Measure Procrastination?

At this point, you should have a clearer idea of what procrastination entails and what is simply some type of necessary or involuntary delay. Using these insights, you may feel that you can get a fairly good idea of your own experiences with delay and whether they qualify as procrastination. But you may also be wondering about the extent to which your procrastination has become a habit for dealing with unpleasant tasks. The "Are You Prone to Procrastination?" exercise (Sirois, Yang, et al., 2019) can help with that. It contains nine statements that researchers like me use when trying to measure people's tendency to procrastinate. After answering each statement with the options presented, score yourself using the instructions. This total score can then be compared against the benchmarks for high, middle, and low levels of procrastination proneness. Keep in mind that these questions measure a tendency to procrastinate on a fairly regular basis, what I refer to as *chronic procrastination.* If you don't procrastinate very often, you will likely have a score in the low range.

EXERCISE: Are You Prone to Procrastination?

Below are some statements that may or may not apply to you. Please give yourself a score for each statement using the guide below. There are no "correct" or "incorrect" answers.

1 False	2 Not usually true for me	3 Sometimes false/true for me	4 Mostly true for me	5 True for me

1. I often find myself performing tasks that I had intended to do days before.	1 2 3 4 5
2. Even with jobs that require little else except sitting down and doing them, I find they seldom get done for days.	1 2 3 4 5

(continues)

3. I generally delay before starting work I have to do.	1	2	3	4	5
4. In preparing for some deadlines, I often waste time by doing other things.	1	2	3	4	5
5. I often have a task finished sooner than necessary.	1	2	3	4	5
6. I usually buy even an essential item at the last minute.	1	2	3	4	5
7. I usually accomplish all the things I plan to do in a day.	1	2	3	4	5
8. I am continually saying "I'll do it tomorrow."	1	2	3	4	5
9. I usually take care of all the tasks I have to do before I settle down and relax for the evening.	1	2	3	4	5

How did you score?

To get your score you will need to first "reverse score" Statements 5, 7, 9 as follows:

Change 1 to 5, 2 to 4, 4 to 2, and 5 to 1.

Next, sum the scores for all items to get a total score, and divide this by 9 to get your average score out of a total score of 5.

Now, check where your average score falls within the categories of chronic procrastination below.

1.0–2.0—Low levels: Whether or not you procrastinate once in awhile, it certainly isn't a regular habit for you.

2.1–3.5—Moderate levels: You probably procrastinate more than you would like to but less than someone for whom procrastination has become a regular habit.

3.6–5.0—High levels: Procrastination is likely your go-to way of dealing with most tasks that you find unpleasant or that trigger negative feelings in you.

Note. From "Development and Validation of the General Procrastination Scale (GPS-9): A Short and Reliable Measure of Trait Procrastination," by F. M. Sirois, S. Yang, and W. van Eerde, 2019, *Personality and Individual Differences, 146,* p. 28 (https://doi.org/10.1016/j.paid.2019.03.039). Copyright 2019 by Elsevier. Adapted with permission.

CAN PROCRASTINATION EVER BE A GOOD THING?

This question comes up a lot when I am speaking with journalists and in interviews with the media. The short answer is "no." The reason why people often think procrastination might not always be detrimental is likely because most of us have delayed something before for a good reason and this delay in turn resulted in a positive outcome. Consider, for example, the situation just described about waiting to write a report until you had all the necessary information. This *delay* was beneficial because it enabled you to write a good report. But it was a delay, *not* procrastination.

Busting the Myth of Active Procrastination

A few years back, a group of researchers introduced the idea of what they termed *active procrastination*, proposing that purposely choosing to procrastinate could actually be positive. In comparison, they suggested that *passive procrastination*, which involved someone putting things off in a less conscious, avoidance-motivated manner, was the harmful form of procrastination (Chu & Choi, 2005). Their idea that some forms of procrastination can be a good thing was picked up very quickly by the media and blogs and heralded as a new understanding of procrastination that cast it in a positive rather than negative light. Of course, this idea was popular: Who wouldn't want to be told that their procrastination was okay and may actually bring rewards?

The problem was that what they were proposing as active procrastination wasn't technically procrastination at all. It was, as you may have guessed already, simply delay, and likely something similar to types of delay I discussed earlier. The researchers described active procrastinators as actively choosing to procrastinate so that they can divert their attention to other more important tasks. Also, these active procrastinators chose to work under pressure until the last minute because they believed doing so enhanced their performance.

REPRIORITIZING ISN'T PROCRASTINATION

This description of an active procrastinator highlights several issues that call into question whether such a form of procrastination actually exists. First, as I just noted, delaying a task so you can shift your focus to more important tasks is delay due to reprioritization of your goals. But this is not procrastination. It would be somewhat foolish to continue to work on one goal when circumstances arise that make another goal more pressing or important. In essence, you would be procrastinating on the goal that should be taking priority if you did not shift your attention to this new goal.

PURPOSEFULLY WAITING UNTIL THE LAST MINUTE ISN'T A SELF-REGULATION FAILURE

The researchers who introduced the idea of active procrastination referred to it as a self-regulation problem (Chu & Choi, 2005). However, as my colleague Tim Pychyl noted in his *Psychology Today* blog, "Don't Delay" (https://www.psychologytoday.com/us/blog/dont-delay), active procrastination can't be both a self-regulation problem and something that people choose to do. That would be akin to saying that people consciously and with full awareness choose to overindulge in cake when they are on a strict diet, or binge drink alcohol, or go on a spending spree when they are on a tight budget. Each of these behaviors reflects a failure in the ability to control your impulses, or self-regulate. The conclusion that active procrastinators would choose to leave things to the last minute because of anticipated benefits is simply illogical.

Procrastinators Know the Consequences of Delay Will Be Bad

This brings us to a third issue with the concept of active procrastination. The assumption is that the choice to leave things to the last minute is driven by an expectation that one's performance will be enhanced because of the rush experienced by working up to the last minute, a rush that will result in more positive outcomes. Think back to the definition provided earlier in this chapter. Included in it is an explicit statement that you can expect negative consequences from the unnecessary and voluntary delay that characterizes procrastination. Active procrastination can't be defined as a form of true procrastination if it results in benefits rather than costs.

Last-Minute Work Will Be Shoddy

The scientific evidence on the outcomes of procrastination, whether chosen or not, do not support the claims that working to the last minute will improve your performance. The bulk of the evidence, from a number of studies, suggests quite the opposite (e.g., Kim & Seo, 2015). Procrastination is associated with poor academic grades and inferior work performance, not better grades and superior performance. It's also likely that what so-called active procrastinators are reporting when they claim to choose to work to the last minute rather than pacing their work is a form of *post hoc rationalization*. Because procrastination is an irrational behavior, if you acknowledge in hindsight that you left things to the last minute, then rationalizing why you would have made this irrational choice serves to protect your self-esteem and ward off any feelings of uneasiness about having procrastinated. You did it with purpose and good reason, so there! Adding in the perception that you actually perform better under such pressure is the icing on the proverbial self-delusion cake.

Although this may sound a bit harsh, consider this: Evidence aside, if it were true that leaving an important task until the last minute is a way for procrastinators to perform better, then why wouldn't they leave *all* their tasks, not only some, to the last minute? Surely taking this approach would be a guaranteed way to write better reports for work, get better academic grades, and so on. But this is rarely, if ever, seen, whether in someone demonstrating actual procrastination or someone engaging in so-called active procrastination.

As you may have started to conclude from our discussion so far, the idea of active procrastination is a bit conceptually messy. It appears to include defining elements that are consistent with regular delay yet distinct from true procrastination. At the same time, it describes behavior, such as working to the last minute, that is very consistent with what we commonly recognize as procrastination.

The Evidence Says Active Procrastination Is a Myth

Other researchers have noticed these inconsistencies and put them to the test. Using a large sample of more than 1,600 students, researchers in Belgium tested whether a self-report questionnaire created to distinguish active from passive procrastination actually did so and whether being an active procrastinator resulted in better academic achievement (Pinxten et al., 2019). Not only did they not find support for the questionnaire measuring procrastination in the way that the original researchers proposed, they also found no evidence to suggest that certain types of procrastinators (i.e., active procrastinators) benefited from purposely delaying their academic tasks. Researchers from Canada also tested whether the concept of active procrastination is valid (Chowdhury & Pychyl, 2018). From the results of their analyses that examined what active procrastination was and wasn't related to, they concluded that active procrastination doesn't include the key defining features of procrastination and therefore is not true

EXERCISE: Can You Spot Who's Procrastinating?

Scenario 1

You've asked your coworker Chris for some information that is critical for a report you are writing. Chris has said they will get it to you by Thursday. It's now Friday, and Chris hasn't replied with the information you needed or updated you about when you can expect it. You have to finish your report by Monday and are feeling time pressured and annoyed with Chris.

Are you procrastinating? Is Chris procrastinating?

Scenario 2

You are trying to come up with a creative solution to a work issue that your boss has asked you to deal with. You're on a tight timeline and have been working steadily for days to try and find a new approach that will work and really wow your boss. But the ideas well is dry, and you feel like time is running out. You decide to recharge your mental batteries by taking a 1-hour break and doing something you enjoy to get your creative juices running again.

Are you procrastinating?

Scenario 3

You've volunteered to put together the newsletter for your local community center. The head of the communications committee sends you a file with all the updates to be included in this month's edition. She informs you that the newsletter needs to be created in a special kind of software to give it a professional look and sends links to online tutorials to help you get started using the software. You've never used this software before and are nervous about whether you can get it to work. A week passes, and you still haven't started the newsletter, which is due to go out in a couple of days.

Are you procrastinating?

procrastination. The takeaway message from all of this is that the idea of active procrastination, although very appealing, especially for those who frequently procrastinate, is not supported by either theory or research and thus can be considered a myth.

Now that we've reviewed descriptions and examples of what is and isn't considered procrastination, this is a good place to practice applying your new knowledge and to clarify your understanding of procrastination. The "Can You Spot Who's Procrastinating?" exercise presents three scenarios that may or may not describe instances of procrastination. Your mission, should you choose to accept it, is to spot who's procrastinating. Vintage pop culture reference aside, it's not an impossible task, but it may be more challenging than you think, so take your time and try to reason through each scenario. The answers, and explanations, appear next.

How did you do? Were you able to spot the procrastinator? If you concluded that Scenario 3 was the only scenario with clear signs of procrastination taking place, then pat yourself on the back: You nailed it. Before we go into examining why only that scenario and not the others reflects procrastination, however, let's unpack the other two scenarios.

In Scenario 1, your coworker Chris is delaying getting back to you with key information you need to write your report, which is preventing you from finishing your report. Because the delay is outside of your control, it isn't voluntary. The delay is also necessary because the missing information is critical to the completion of your report. So no, you are not procrastinating.

But what about Chris? Chris said they would get you the information, so an intention was made. But Chris hasn't followed through, so there is a delay. The critical question is whether Chris's delay is voluntary or necessary. The problem is that we can't tell why Chris has delayed getting back to you, whether there was a good reason for the delay. Without this information it is impossible to tell whether Chris is procrastinating or delaying with good reason because of circumstances or influences beyond their control. The correct answer here is we don't know whether Chris is procrastinating. In fact, in many situations it can be difficult to tell whether someone else is procrastinating or simply delaying. We simply do not always have the information needed to make that judgment call. In such cases it may be better to err on the side of caution, and compassion, and assume that it is delay until further information comes to light.

Scenario 2 involves pausing (delaying?) the pursuit of a solution for your boss. The timelines are tight, but you choose to delay working on this by 1 hour, so the delay is voluntary. Is the delay necessary, or perhaps even wise? Most likely it is both, given that you are no longer working efficiently, and your creative thinking isn't at its best. Taking the break, which is only an hour, has purpose. You are not trying to avoid working on the solution for your boss; instead, you want to replenish your mental resources so that you can complete the task to a good standard. In short, you are lacking something you need to finish the work (a fresh perspective), so you choose to delay and do something that will help you get what you need to complete the task. So, in this scenario there is no evidence of procrastination, only sagacious delay.

In contrast to the first two scenarios, the delay in Scenario 3 fits our definition of procrastination quite well. There is a clear intent to complete the task—you volunteered to help with the newsletter, after all. The delay described is unnecessary and voluntary. Even though you are unfamiliar with the software needed to create the newsletter, you have been given the resources necessary to learn and use it. Thus, you can't claim that you are delaying because you were missing critical information. It appears that the main reason for avoiding starting the newsletter is a feeling of nervousness about using a software you are unfamiliar with, despite being given tutorials to learn how to use it. Sounds irrational, right? That is because it is indeed irrational and because there are unpleasant emotions involved that are driving the delay.

WHY DO WE PROCRASTINATE?

The definition of procrastination we unpacked earlier in this chapter provides a solid basis for understanding what is and what isn't procrastination. It can help you discern between more general delay and true procrastination because it highlights that the actions or tasks being delayed are ones that you stated an intention to do and that if you are delaying those tasks it's not because someone asked you to do so or because a delay was caused by an unexpected crisis and thus necessary. It also acknowledges that true procrastination has negative consequences and involves an awareness that this unnecessary delay will not be beneficial for you or others.

Although this definition is useful, it doesn't point us in a clear direction about the causes of procrastination and in turn how best to manage and reduce procrastination. This is one of the main reasons that I, along with my colleague and friend Tim Pychyl, proposed an extension to this standard definition of procrastination in a theoretical article we authored on the topic (Sirois & Pychyl, 2013). The idea was not to replace the basic definition but to elaborate on it in a way that would better highlight what we view as the underlying processes and causes involved in procrastination. Our new definition reads as follows: "Procrastination is a form of self-regulation failure that involves prioritizing short-term mood repair over the long-term pursuit of intended actions."

You'll notice that this definition includes several of the same elements as the traditional one. For example, it notes that procrastination involves self-regulation failure, and it also mentions that the actions being delayed are ones that were intended. But there are also some important new elements in this definition that speak to what we proposed are the underlying or core causes of procrastination, namely difficulties in mood regulation.

A central theme in this definition is the idea that procrastination involves putting more importance on trying to repair or change your immediate mood than simply getting on with what needs to get done. In short, we procrastinate to avoid the negative feelings associated with a task, but we do so at the expense of following through and completing our task. Avoiding the task also helps us put it conveniently out of our thoughts—out of sight, out of mind, as they say. However, as I discuss in later chapters, trying to suppress our thoughts and emotions this way can actually backfire: It can make us more focused on the task we are trying to avoid and feel worse as well.

From this view, procrastination seems quite irrational. Why would anyone risk not achieving important personal, work, relationship, financial, or health goals simply so that they can feel a little bit better now? To answer to this important question, and find ways to reduce procrastination, we need to turn to psychological science. Research findings in this field offer insights into the processes underlying the struggles people face that can lead them to procrastinate. This is the focus of Chapters 2 through 4. Chapters 5 and 6 outline in depth why emotions play such a key role in procrastination, and Chapters 7 through 10 then translate these insights into evidence-based approaches and strategies you can use to change your habits and procrastinate less.

CHAPTER 2

THAT MYSTICAL LAND OF TOMORROW: LOST PRODUCTIVITY AND ABANDONED DREAMS

Tomorrow is a mystical land where 99 percent of all human productivity, motivation, and achievement is stored.

—Anonymous

In this chapter, you will learn

- how procrastination can lead to other problem behaviors;
- how to recognize when you may be procrastinating at work or in your academic life; and
- how procrastination takes a toll on your financial well-being, motivation, and daily happiness, even in the moments when you aren't procrastinating.

It's hard to estimate the overall costs of unfulfilled dreams and abandoned goals due to procrastination, but there are some good examples that illustrate these costs in concrete terms. Each year, more than 50% of people who sign up for gym memberships abandon them within 6 months, which amounts to an estimated waste of $49 million per year (Shaw, 2011). Other research, conducted with more than 2,000 full-time employees, found that, on average, people waste about 4 hours a day procrastinating rather than doing their work tasks (Human Resources Online, 2020). As you can imagine, this procrastination translates into significant losses in productivity and financial losses for employers as well as lost opportunities for career advancement for the employees. These are just a couple of examples of the known financial costs of procrastinating. Add to these late fines for overdue bills and tax returns, as well as unwanted purchases that can't be returned because the refund date has passed, and it becomes clear that the financial costs can be quite substantial and concerning.

There are also other, less noticeable but equally concerning, costs to abandoning or not reaching our goals. Decades of research have clearly shown that having and working toward goals are important parts of life. The goals we set direct our choices and the actions we take. Some would argue that they are also an important part of how we define ourselves and express ourselves in the world. Whether it's working toward being a better parent, becoming a healthier version of ourselves, or developing professional skills so we can excel in our career, the goals we work toward say a lot about us and what we value in our lives. After all, working toward goals requires a conscious investment of effort and time, both of which are limited resources. Big or small, goals are crucial to our health and well-being, and not being able to reach goals because of procrastination can have profound and far-reaching effects on our lives.

In the next three chapters, we take a closer look at some of the costs of procrastination and the areas of our lives where unnecessary delay of intended tasks can take a toll. In this chapter, we start by examining how and why procrastination can wreak havoc in the workplace and with academic goals. We also focus in on ways to get better at noticing when you may be procrastinating at work or in your academic life so that you can nip any tendencies in the bud before they get out of hand. In the chapters that follow, we examine the toll procrastination can take on physical and mental health and on our professional and personal relationships.

Before we go any further, I want to make it clear that the aim of looking at the costs of procrastination is not to "blame and shame," as they say. That would be counterproductive. Increasing any negative feelings we have about our procrastination is a sure way to feed into further procrastination and thus not a very good approach for trying to reduce it. Recall that in Chapter 1, I introduced the ideas that short-term mood repair lies at the core of procrastination and that we procrastinate as a way of avoiding the negative mood we experience as being linked to a task. We unpack this idea more fully in Chapters 5 and 6. For now, though, it's safe to say that it's important to make you aware of the consequences of procrastination while not making you feel worse than you may already feel. Becoming aware of and understanding the consequences of procrastination can help us take a more accountable and compassionate view of our procrastination rather than minimizing or avoiding its toll. Learning to view our behavior and its consequences in an objective and accepting manner, rather than being judgmental or reactive, can be challenging, especially if we don't like what we see, but it's an important first step if we want to change things. Admitting the costs of our procrastination can in turn lay the foundation for understanding where procrastination may be having the most impact on our lives so that we can target those areas first and start to regain control and get back on track with our dreams and goals.

I'LL GET TO MY ACADEMIC WORK, LATER

In Chapter 1, we talked about how prevalent procrastination is among college and university students. To continue on that theme, a number of studies have shown that students who procrastinate are more likely to engage in academic misconduct and use of a variety of unfair means to avoid the inevitable consequences of having put off studying or working on assignments to the last minute. One of the largest and most comprehensive of these studies was conducted by researchers in Germany (Patrzek et al., 2015). They asked more than 3,000 students from four different universities to report the extent to which they procrastinated on their academic tasks and how often they used unfair means to complete their work. The students were queried initially and 6 months later in an online survey.

What the researchers found was shocking, yet somewhat expected given what we know about procrastination: Of the students, 75% reported engaging in at least one form of academic misconduct. However, students who reported procrastinating on their academic work in the first survey were also more likely than those who did not procrastinate to engage in one or more forms of academic misconduct over the next 6 months. In particular, procrastinating students frequently used fraudulent excuses and misused medical certificates to extend deadlines for their work. This makes sense if we consider that, as the amount of time left to complete work or study decreases, the time pressure experienced by the student increases. This has been referred to as the *deadline effect*. Other research has shown that gaining extra time is a common reason for using fraudulent excuses to extend deadlines and make up for time lost due to procrastination. So, in some ways, it's not surprising the procrastinating students used this strategy most often.

Dishonesty and Excuses?

The student procrastinators did not limit their academic misconduct to only using bogus excuses; in fact, they were also more likely to use a variety of different dishonest means over the 6-month period of the study. These students also engaged in a number of forms of cheating and plagiarism, including copying from other students during exams or on assignments, sneaking crib notes into exams, and even falsifying data for reports. In short, they resorted to any means that would reduce their risk of getting poor grades.

On the surface, it can be easy to condemn these dishonest behaviors. After all, using these fraudulent means to boost grades on assignments and exams that would have otherwise been poor, or even failing, is unfair to all the students who didn't procrastinate and who put honest and timely effort into their academic work. Putting aside the apparent issues with a compromised moral compass, it's been suggested that students who procrastinate view these unfair means as an adaptive way of coping with the pressing demands of this situation. In the panic of the moment, when their grades are on the line, they literally think "Do whatever it takes to get a good grade," or face failure, quite literally. So, although we may not condone this questionable way of coping, we can certainly understand the reasons for it and perhaps not judge it too harshly.

. . . Or Simply Coping?

The problem with the above approach is that it focuses on immediate outcomes and not the long-term costs. Getting the assignment done, or not failing the exam, takes priority over the process of learning and bettering oneself and one's career prospects and ignores the potential consequences of getting caught. In many institutions of higher education academic misconduct and using unfair means come with a hefty cost, ranging from large grade penalties, to failing the course, to even expulsion. There are a number of reasons why we tend to focus on the immediate situation instead of the big picture when we are chasing down deadlines because we have procrastinated, including the effects that stress has on our thinking. I discuss these in more depth in Chapter 5.

Postgraduate students are not immune to the costs of academic procrastination. Research on procrastination among master's and doctoral students has found that unnecessary delay can translate into poorer performance on courses and group assignments (Jiao et al., 2011). Postgraduate students who struggle with procrastination are also at higher risk for taking longer to complete, or even not completing, their degree, mainly because they put off writing up their thesis or dissertation. The following example from a graduate student highlights some of the all-too-common issues students encounter during work on their dissertation:

> The whole dissertation process has been full of procrastination. At the very beginning, I found it incredibly difficult to get started because it was such a mammoth task, and I didn't know where to start. The aspect of the work I procrastinated most on was the writing because this seemed the most arduous. I also found that when a particular aspect of writing was difficult, I procrastinated more. Now as I am coming toward the end of my dissertation time, I'm getting quite stressed, which makes me procrastinate even more.

This example provides important insights into the vicious cycle of procrastinating and then feeling bad about doing so. This cycle can unfortunately mean that the dissertation isn't completed on time. If we considered only the objective aspects of the student's procrastination—not writing up the dissertation in a timely manner—it would be easy to be critical and perhaps judge the student as being lazy or just slacking off. But if we consider their subjective experience and internal struggles of writing up their dissertation and how this promoted procrastination, then it becomes apparent that there is more than meets the eye. From this perspective, it's a little easier to have some compassion for their struggles and suffering.

When postgraduate students do manage to finish writing up and passing their thesis or dissertation, many often do so well beyond the normal time limits. As you can imagine, this isn't very promising in regard to job prospects. What employer would want to hire someone who took an unusually long period of time to finish their postgraduate degree when they could instead hire someone who finished on time?

Unfortunately, these are the sort of demotivating thoughts students may have that can actually make finishing even harder.

SOLDIERING, CYBERSLACKING, AND OTHER GARDEN VARIETY FORMS OF WORKPLACE PROCRASTINATION

What about the costs of procrastination in the workplace? At the beginning of this chapter I alluded to the enormous financial costs of procrastination for employers. Some estimates suggest that employees can spend up to a quarter of their working day procrastinating instead of working (Davies, 2017). This loss in productivity can translate to an annual cost for employers of anywhere between $8,000 and $10,000, on average, per employee. If you multiply that cost by, say, 100 employees, you are looking at procrastination costing an employer about $1,000,000 a year.

It's clear that workplace procrastination can have a significant financial impact on employers. But what about the costs for employees? Although most of the research on the impact of procrastination on performance and reaching goals has been conducted with students, there is a growing interest in understanding procrastination in the workplace, the different forms it can take, and how it can affect employees.

What do people do when they procrastinate at work? According to researchers in the Netherlands, workplace procrastination can come in one of two forms, each with its own set of costs (Metin et al., 2016). The first type of workplace procrastination involves offline activities that people do instead of their work, for example, taking an extended coffee or lunch break, spending time gossiping and socializing outside of breaks, and daydreaming instead of working. Engaging in these offline activities instead of work for more than 1 hour a day is referred to as *soldiering*. This term was first coined back in 1911 to refer to *underworking,* or working so slowly so that you could, in effect, avoid a full day's work. It may have come from some people's tendency to "just put in my time" during required years of national service. Since then, organizational psychologists have adopted the term *soldiering* to refer to when people delay work simply for the sake of delaying work rather than because they intentionally want to cause harm to others in the workplace or to their employer.

This type of work-avoiding is most likely to happen when employees don't strongly identify with their job and don't feel a strong ethical obligation to work when they should. In short, employees may feel bored or underchallenged by their work tasks, which can be experienced as unpleasantness. Disengaging from their work by doing other, more pleasant activities provides some relief from these feelings; however, the quick fix afforded by soldiering comes at a cost. Soldiering is linked to underperformance in the workplace, which in turn can result in lost opportunities for career advancement.

The second type of workplace procrastination has emerged as a result of the increased use of technology at work. *Cyberslacking* is a relatively new form of procrastinating at work that involves using online activities to avoid work tasks. If you've ever paused your work to check your social media feed, read a cooking blog, check your instant messages or texts, play an online game, surf the web, or shop online when not on a lunch or work break, then you've cyberslacked. Don't feel too bad if you have, though: According to a survey of more 1,000 employees in the United States who do computer-based work, four out of five admit to having used the internet for personal reasons during work at some point. Moreover, a survey of employees found that 97% of men and 85% of women feel that cyberslacking is an acceptable behavior at work (V. K. G. Lim & Chen, 2012).

These high rates of cyberslacking may seem a bit shocking, but if you consider how easy it is to cyberslack at work then it's understandable why so many employees do it and think that it is okay. Take easy access to a computer and the internet, add a dash of giving the impression that you are researching something for work when you are really shopping for a birthday gift, and a sprinkle of the magic of juggling multiple browser tabs, and you have the perfect recipe for cyberslacking. Barring any software that may be installed to track your internet use, cyberslacking most likely will go unnoticed by your boss. And if you are lucky enough to work independently, or at home, as many more people do these days, without anyone to monitor your work, you may identify with the following example from an academic struggling to get their grading done:

> Several undergraduate theses to mark over a recent weekend. Sat down at my desk in reasonably good time to start them. Immediately jumped on Facebook, YouTube, Wikipedia . . . you name it. Got [to] the first one half an hour later. Regular checks of emails throughout the first thesis. Another big "break" in between the first and second one. Gave up after the latter.

Most researchers (and employers) view cyberslacking as a harmful work behavior that reduces employee productivity, but it can also have other, more significant costs. When employees spend time on nonsecure sites and watch funny cat videos on YouTube while they are cyberslacking, network performance and security can be compromised. This can also translate into extra costs for removing malware and viruses from visiting these sites. In fact, it's been estimated that cyberslacking costs companies about $130,000 per year for dealing with the technical aftermath of cyberslacking. Note that this is in addition to the costs due to lost productivity. Although a couple of minutes here and there spent on the internet for personal reasons during work time may not seem like much, when considered cumulatively it can amount to a significant loss in productivity.

Are You Taking a Healthy Mental Break?

Despite these costs, there is some debate as to whether cyberslacking, or *cyberloafing*, as it is often referred to, is really all that harmful. Some researchers and employers believe that there are more benefits than costs to letting employees take pauses from work to engage in personal online activities such as gaming, checking social media, or online shopping. Advocates of these breaks suggest that they provide important opportunities for employees to mentally recharge that can translate into better productivity, creative thinking, and renewed motivation and enthusiasm for work. Taking breaks in general provides psychological detachment from work that can be beneficial for gaining perspective on one's work and reenergizing thinking processes. We all need to take a break at times because there are limits to the amount of time we can spend working on the same task and still be effective. Five minutes of watching funny cat videos may help you feel reenergized to get that report finished. From this perspective, cyberslacking would appear to be beneficial for employees. But if cyberslacking is a form of workplace procrastination, and procrastination by definition is harmful, then how can cyberslacking be beneficial?

This question is why some researchers suggest that using the term *cyberslacking* to refer to all instances of using work time for online activities is inappropriate. They suggest instead that "personal internet use" is a better phrase that doesn't have the negative connotations cyberslacking does. Personal internet use can be beneficial or, when it takes the form of cyberslacking, harmful. As a procrastination researcher, I am in complete agreement with this distinction. We need to be careful to not confuse taking healthy mental breaks at work, whatever form they take, with workplace procrastination; otherwise, we can fool ourselves into thinking that all that gaming, internet shopping, and social media use while at work is just fine and become blind to the costs of procrastination to ourselves and others.

So, how can we tell the difference between when a break to read our favorite blog is a healthy mental break and when it is cyberslacking? On the surface, taking a mental refresher may look very similar to cyberslacking, which is exactly why the two are often confused. However, there are two features of cyberslacking that make it distinct from other personal uses of the internet at work. The first involves the amount of time you spend engaged in internet activities. There's arguably a fine line between what constitutes a reasonable amount of time spent surfing the internet or watching videos to refocus between tasks and what can be considered to be excessive and likely reflect an avoidance of work. Although there is no hard-and-fast rule as to how much time is too much, most experts agree that from 10 to no more than 20 minutes is usually sufficient to achieve psychological detachment and a healthy mental reset so that you will be more focused and productive when you return to your work.

Monitoring how much time you spend on the internet at work for personal reasons is one useful, albeit crude, way of recognizing when your mental break may be turning into cyberslacking. When your breaks become more frequent and last longer than the time spent on your work, then it's probably a safe bet you are cyberslacking. The following example describes a working pattern that is dominated by procrastination:

> I was required to write some copy for my job, and found that every time I set out to do it I would open the document and get everything ready to go, and then just open Facebook or an equally unimportant/uninteresting and unrelated web page and browse for some time, periodically going back and looking over the work and perhaps writing a few words before taking another of these fairly long "breaks." I felt ashamed every time I did it, but I got into a routine of doing [it] so regularly, sometimes for whole days, where I would go home feeling that I had done almost no work and feeling bad about myself.

On the surface, it seems illogical that someone would actually continue to cyberslack even when they feel so bad about it afterward, but this is the trap of procrastination. The immediate rewards we get from avoiding an unpleasant or challenging work task outweigh the emotional aftermath of procrastinating, something we don't often think about in that moment we decide to procrastinate.

Take a Moment

Let's pause to think about your own possible experiences with cyberslacking. Ask yourself: When have I used the internet at work for personal reasons? What websites or social media sites did I visit? Was I taking a needed or scheduled break, or was I trying to avoid work?

. . . Or Looking for Relief From Boredom, Anxiety, or Stress?

To be more accurate in detecting whether you are slipping into workplace procrastination, you also need to consider the motives underlying taking that "quick" internet break. Are you taking a break because you need to clear your head and allow your ideas to gel a bit so that you can work more effectively when you return, or are you taking a break because you want relief from the frustration, boredom, anxiety, or stress of your work? If it's the former, then it's most likely that the internet break will be constructive and perhaps even boost your productivity, but if the reason you are taking an internet break is to provide relief from uncomfortable or unpleasant feelings linked to your work, it's likely that you are cyberslacking.

Research largely confirms this idea. Results from a survey of employees conducted by a multinational team of researchers from the United States, Canada, and Korea found that about three quarters of employees who felt they were not treated fairly at work admitted to cyberslacking (Kim et al., 2016). Although feeling mistreated at work may not be directly linked to a specific task, such feelings of perceived injustice can be pervasive and taint the perception of any work-related tasks, making them unpleasant enough that we want to avoid them. Other researchers have similarly noted that feelings of boredom, and a general lack of satisfaction with one's work or work environment, make it more likely that people will cyberslack (Metin et al., 2016).

It's worth mentioning here that much of what we've discussed about cyberslacking and its causes can also apply to academic work. Taking so-called breaks from studying, working on assignments, or writing up a dissertation report by spending time on the internet or social media outlets qualifies as cyberslacking if the reasons for the break are not purely for a mental refresh. When you use the internet as an escape from difficulties with your academic work, or from other unpleasant feelings that emerge as you struggle with academic tasks, this too is a form of procrastination.

How Do You Know If You Are Taking a Healthy Break Versus Procrastinating?

Decision trees are useful tools to help detect issues in decisions and behavior. If you've ever used an online symptom checker to understand your medical issues, then you've used a decision tree. The decision tree in Figure 2.1 is based on the research on work-related procrastination. You can use it as a starting point to help you identify whether your break from work, including academic work, may be procrastination rather than a healthy mental break. Once you've answered the questions in this decision tree, you can then review the questions in the Exercise, "Is It a Break or Procrastination?", at the end of this chapter, to dig deeper and gain some insight and understanding of when and why you might be procrastinating on your work or academic tasks.

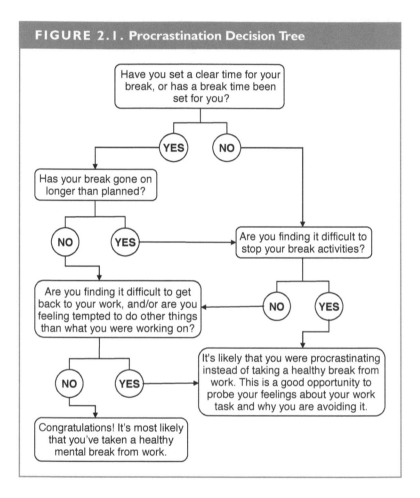

FIGURE 2.1. Procrastination Decision Tree

CAN CHRONIC PROCRASTINATION AFFECT YOUR CAREER PROSPECTS?

Up to this point we have discussed workplace procrastination, the different forms it can take, and how to spot when and why a break from your work might be turning into procrastination. We've also reviewed the potential costs of workplace procrastination for employers. But what about the costs to the individual? Apart from the immediate costs of possibly experiencing guilt about procrastinating on your work, and falling behind on tasks, are there any other costs? The answer, in short, is "yes."

According to an online survey of more than 22,000 employees, when procrastination becomes a chronic tendency at work there are several very real, negative consequences that can have long-term harmful impacts on one's career goals (Kim et al., 2016). The researchers examined how employees' levels of chronic procrastination were associated with a variety of work-related factors, such as income, length and stability of employment, and the type of job they held. The results painted a fairly bleak picture for those who chronically procrastinated: Not only did people who chronically procrastinate have lower annual incomes, they also tended to have less stable employment profiles. Compared with employees who did not procrastinate, procrastinators tended to be employed for shorter periods, work part time rather than full time, and were more likely to be unemployed.

This evidence underscores the potentially serious consequences that poor productivity and performance can have for career advancement. Workplaces and job markets can be fiercely competitive. People who are productive and perform well tend to advance; those who are not are left in the proverbial dust. And if we consider the significant costs incurred by employers from workplace procrastination, it makes sense why employment instability would be linked to a tendency to procrastinate.

These were not the only impacts of being a chronic procrastinator noted by the researchers. People who regularly procrastinated were also likely to hold jobs that were unchallenging, had few opportunities for autonomy, and did not require strong motivational or organizational skills. In other words, people who were prone to procrastinate tended to be drawn to jobs that did not require much self-discipline, and such jobs tended to be ones that paid less or that held less inner value for the person.

What all of this suggests is that people who chronically procrastinate may end up in jobs with which they are not happy and that may not allow them to fulfill their personal career goals or offer opportunities for advancement. Unfortunately, these consequences of work-related procrastination can feed into a vicious circle of further procrastination when it comes to trying to change jobs. The following example from someone who found themselves in an unfulfilling job illustrates this point well:

> I would really like a new job; I am the unhappiest I can possibly be in my current job. I applied for another job and was interviewed a couple of times. I felt bad about myself and inadequate that I wasn't offered the job, and I put off applying for another job before a deadline—even though getting a new job is what I really, really want and a solution to my current work problem.

This example highlights how even taking steps that would provide a solution to the unhappiness with a current job becomes difficult for someone who struggles with procrastination. As we discuss in the following chapters, procrastination in work and other contexts can take a toll on our well-being, and this can then feed into our tendencies to further procrastinate.

Although the consequences of procrastination we've discussed to this point may all sound discouraging, there is hope. If you can understand when and why you procrastinate, even with important work-related or academic tasks, then you can decide which approaches are best suited to tackling your own procrastination. Armed with this evidence-based knowledge, you can target the core reasons for your procrastination and set up our tasks and environments in ways that support your goals and reduce your temptation to procrastinate.

EXERCISE: Is It a Break or Procrastination?

This guided activity can help you gain a better understanding of when and why your breaks from your work or academic tasks might turn into procrastination.

Prebreak Thoughts and Feelings

Reasons

Question: Why do you want to take a break? Try to be honest with yourself and try not to judge your reasons.

Taking a break because you need to mentally refresh and clear your thoughts is a good sign that your break will be a healthy one. If you're taking a break to avoid unpleasant feelings linked to your work task because it's unpleasant or boring, or it triggers negative thoughts and feelings about yourself or your abilities, then this is a good opportunity to explore those thoughts and feelings in a kind and accepting way.

Activity

Question: What do you plan to do on your break? Is it an activity that you will find easy to stop once you get going?

If it is not, you may want to reconsider your choice of break activities and choose something that you know you can disengage from more easily when your break is over.

Timing

Question: Have you put something in place, such as a timer, to help you monitor how much time you are spending on your break?

It can be easy to get lost in break activities and lose track of time, especially if you are experiencing difficulties with your work. Using tools to help you monitor your break time can help support your intentions to not let your break turn into procrastination.

(continues)

EXERCISE: Is It a Break or Procrastination?
(*Continued*)

During-Break Thoughts and Feelings

Mood Check

Question: Are you enjoying your break, or do you find that you are feeling guilty or bad about taking a break?

Although feeling bad could be a sign of overworking and not allowing yourself to take healthy breaks, feeling bad while taking a break can also be a signal that you may be avoiding work you know you should be doing.

Lost in the Moment?

Question: Are you losing track of time while on your break, perhaps because you are becoming too absorbed in your break activities?

Being "in the moment" with your break activities can be healthy in that it helps promote psychological detachment from work, which can be refreshing. However, this can go too far when absorption in your break activity becomes an escape from work and reasonable time limits.

When the End Is Near

Question: Are you finding it difficult to stop your break activities and return to work? Are you having feelings of dread as you think about going back to work?

Healthy breaks from work will usually leave you feeling more motivated to return to work rather than dreading getting back to work. Although it's natural to feel a bit of disappointment when an enjoyable break is over, if an urge to avoid work remains as the end of your break nears, this may be a sign that there are bigger issues at hand. Being aware of these feelings is the first step toward identifying any issues with your work that may be making you want to avoid it and procrastinate.

EXERCISE: Is It a Break or Procrastination?
(Continued)

Postbreak Thoughts and Feelings

Feelings

Question: How do you feel after taking a break? Do you feel refreshed, alert or focused, and enthusiastic to get back to your work, or do you feel drained, or even anxious, about returning to your work and regret that your break is over?

Actions

Question: After your break, do you get back to your work task right away, or do you find yourself finding other things to do instead, such as checking email, chatting with colleagues, or engaging in other low-importance tasks?

If you find yourself finding excuses to do other, less important things than the work task that you took a break from, it could be a sign that you are procrastinating. There's a difference between being busy and being productive. Getting busy with nonessential tasks is another way to avoid the important work task that you should be doing now that your break is over.

CHAPTER 3

CAN PROCRASTINATION BE BAD FOR YOUR HEALTH?

Time and health are two precious assets that we don't recognize and appreciate until they have been depleted.
—Denis Waitley

In this chapter, you will learn

- how and why procrastination can affect mental health;
- the different ways procrastination can be harmful for physical health; and
- how to become more aware of how procrastination affects your mental and physical health and what you can do about it.

It was back in 2001 that I was first introduced to the idea that procrastination may have consequences for health. As a doctoral student in health psychology at Carleton University I had the good fortune to meet Dr. Tim Pychyl, arguably one of the world's leading experts, then and now, on the topic of procrastination. Tim was a member of the psychology department at that time, and his Procrastination Research Group site was the go-to resource for information, research, and even comics, on procrastination.

Knowing that my research interests were in the area of health and well-being, Tim thought that a recent research article suggesting that procrastination is linked to higher stress and poor physical health in students may be of interest to me. It was the first study to suggest a link between procrastination and poor health. As a budding health psychologist with a strong interest in personality science, I was of course intrigued by the idea and the findings. Who would have thought that a behavior as common procrastination, that is often laughed off as being trivial, could actually be bad for your health?

Inspired by this initial research study, I had to know more. Although what the researchers had found was intriguing, a number of unanswered questions remained. Given how prevalent procrastination is among students, is it harmful to the health only of students, or are other adults vulnerable to the health-harming effects of procrastination? Could procrastination be harmful for health in ways other than simply reporting more physical symptoms and having higher self-reported stress? Most important, why might procrastination be bad for your health? It was these questions that launched my ongoing research program into procrastination and health. After 20 years (at the time of this writing) of researching these and other related questions, I've discovered that procrastination is indeed bad for your health in numerous and often surprising ways. Understanding these consequences for mental and physical health is the focus of this chapter.

THE TOLL OF PROCRASTINATION ON MENTAL HEALTH

On the surface, it can be hard to imagine how simply putting off a task can contribute to poor mental health, including anxiety, stress, depression, and general distress. When you unnecessarily delay doing something important that you know you should be doing, you can certainly feel bad about it. Perhaps you feel a bit of guilt or even shame if your procrastination is apparent to others. Or maybe you feel stressed and worry about what will happen if you don't complete the task on time.

According to research, these are exactly the types of emotional reactions people experience when they procrastinate. Numerous studies have demonstrated that procrastinating on important and intended tasks can lead people to experience a range of negative thoughts and emotions, including guilt, shame, stress, anxiety, depression, self-loathing, and feelings of incompetency (e.g., Sirois & Pychyl, 2013). Any of these feelings on their own are well known to be harmful to well-being, but consider also that when you procrastinate on a task, acknowledging that you are procrastinating doesn't always put an end to your delay right away. Experiencing these negative feelings can drive further procrastination because you now feel even worse about the task than you did initially. I drill down into these ideas even further in Chapter 5.

If left unchecked, these negative responses to procrastination can quickly turn into a cycle of procrastination and poor mental health. This is why procrastination of an initial and sometimes small task can snowball out of control into a situation that is either unsalvageable or has a significant impact on well-being. This can happen for even everyday tasks.

It's fairly common for most homeowners to feel the need to make home improvements at some point. Not surprisingly, a whole retail industry has flourished over the past few decades to support homeowners who want to take on their own home improvement tasks. But it's also common for many homeowners to procrastinate starting or finishing these renovations or repairs. Home improvements can be daunting at the best of times, especially given that the scope of the project can easily become larger than expected. It's no surprise, then, that procrastinating on home improvements was a common theme among people whom I asked to share their stories of procrastination.

Consider the example that follows. Fear and worry about what might be discovered when the work started was enough to drive this person to put off starting some needed home improvement work.

These feelings then turned into dread and anxiety and were allowed to fester as the procrastination continued:

> I needed to draught proof the holes in my living room floor. I put it off because it makes me worried about living in an inadequate house. I was scared I would find something that would require some work . . . that I was unable to do myself. I felt dread and anxiety.

In the next example, we can also understand how initially procrastinating challenging home renovations might lead to weeks of delay and, eventually, feelings of depression:

> I've been meaning to do a lot of modifications to my house for some time, but they are generally quite difficult and time consuming and I keep delaying, saying "I'll do it next week." I really intend to do it but constantly do not have the effort to see it through, and this causes me to get somewhat depressed.

These examples illustrate how procrastination can be bookended by negative feelings. First, we feel bad about the task. Then we feel bad about not being able to move forward and take action. As you can imagine, if your negative feelings about doing home improvements is what prompted you to procrastinate in the first place, then feeling bad about not doing them is more likely to promote, rather than resolve, your procrastination. If your procrastination continues, then it is likely your mental health will take a hit as well.

But can these negative emotional responses to procrastination turn into full-blown feelings of depression, anxiety, and general distress? If so, how? In the examples of procrastinating on home improvements, feelings of anxiety and distress were tied to the one task and not being able to take action on it. Now imagine that this dynamic of procrastinating and then feeling distress about the procrastination is happening not just for one task or area of your life but for several. If finances, work, health activities, relationships, and other personal goals are being procrastinated from time to time, and each time you feel distress, it's not hard to imagine how the cumulative effect of this procrastination could, over time, add up to poor mental health.

The scenario I have just described refers specifically to effects on mental health that we might expect when we habitually procrastinate. If you recall, this type of chronic, widespread procrastination can be thought of as a personality trait. It characterizes and often dominates the way a person responds to tasks that are less than pleasant or that provoke negative thoughts and feelings. It makes sense that if you procrastinate frequently, and across a variety of different tasks, then the risk for experiencing sustained mental health difficulties most likely will increase.

Research on how and why procrastination is linked to depression and anxiety supports this idea, but it's possible that this is a chicken-and-egg effect. Chronic procrastination can contribute to symptoms of depression and anxiety. When we fail to reach our goals, we can feel depressed or anxious about lost opportunities. But people who are depressed and anxious are also more likely to procrastinate. This makes sense if we consider what happens to people's motivation when they are feeling depressed. Their motivation to pursue goals is low, as is their tolerance for any setbacks. If they experience challenges, then these might be viewed as confirming negative beliefs about their abilities, whether they are deserving of success, and so on. Anxiety about the task not being completed up to a certain standard, or about making mistakes, can also lead to task avoidance. And when people are feeling anxious or depressed, this backdrop of negative emotions can make minor negative feelings about a task loom larger. The result is that unpleasant tasks that might normally be tolerated are now avoided. In short, procrastination can feed into feelings of anxiety and depression, which can in turn make it easier to procrastinate.

I'll Go to Therapy, Later

From our discussion so far it should be fairly clear that when procrastination becomes a regular way of dealing with unpleasant or aversive tasks, mental health can suffer. The best course of action when this happens is to seek help from a mental health professional. In recent years, researchers and clinicians have identified a number of effective therapies for managing the thoughts and emotions that underpin a tendency to procrastinate, so there is indeed help available for dealing with procrastination and its impact on your mental health.

But wait a minute. If you are someone who is prone to procrastination, what are the chances that you won't also procrastinate on seeking help for your mental health issues? This is exactly the question that a group of researchers from Canada set out to answer (Stead et al., 2010). They asked undergraduate students to report their levels of chronic procrastination and stress as well as any mental health issues they were experiencing. They also asked whether the students had spoken to a mental health professional or sought help for their mental health concerns.

What they found was both unsurprising and concerning: Students who were chronic procrastinators reported experiencing higher levels of stress and poorer mental health. In fact, it was the combination of chronic procrastination and stress together that contributed to having more mental health issues. Perhaps more concerning, though, is that those who were prone to procrastination were—you guessed it—less likely to have sought help for their poor mental health. The very students who were most in need of help to deal with their mental health were the least likely to seek it. Their procrastination extended to putting off dealing with their mental health.

What if we turn these results around and view them from another angle? This evidence would then also suggest that when you reduce your tendency to procrastinate and manage your stress (which are of course strongly linked), then your mental health will improve, and you will be also be more likely to seek help for any mental health concerns you may have. In this same study, the researchers noted that the presence of chronic procrastination was the main barrier to seeking help (Stead et al., 2010). Students with poor mental health were more likely to speak to a therapist or mental health nurse if they were not prone to procrastination.

Procrastination and the Trap of Social Media

The activities people choose to do when they are procrastinating can also aggravate their negative mood. If the aim of procrastination is to reduce or remove the negative mood you experience from unpleasant or threatening tasks, then doing something more pleasant or distracting will help accomplish this and provide you with a quick, albeit temporary, mood boost. Using the internet and social media are easy ways to achieve the short-term mood repair that we seek when we are procrastinating. In addition to the research on cyberslacking we discussed in the last chapter, a number of research studies have shown that people very often use social media as way of procrastinating (e.g., Meier et al., 2016).

One of the reasons that using social media to procrastinate is so popular is because of the immediate boost in positive feelings that we can get. Watching cute cat videos on YouTube or TikTok can almost certainly put a smile on your face, evoke a much-needed laugh or giggle, or give you a jolt of joy. But, like any quick emotional fix, the effects of consuming this enjoyable form of social media are often fleeting, quickly replaced by the original unpleasant feelings that drove you to seek out this distraction in the first place. But there can be additional costs as well.

My use of watching cat videos as an example of social media procrastination is not by accident (or personal preference). Believe it or not, there has actually been research conducted on what happens when people watch cute cat videos when they procrastinate. In one study, researchers surveyed nearly 6,800 people about their internet cat video viewing habits and whether these habits were linked to procrastination (Myrick, 2015). What they found highlighted one of the key differences between healthy and unhealthy breaks that we explored in Chapter 2. For most people, watching fluffy, sweet kittens and cats climbing curtains, getting tangled in yarn, or putting the family dog in its place was harmless. It provided them with much-needed stress relief and humor and functioned as a healthy and effective break.

However, this was not the case for those watched internet cat videos as a way of procrastinating. For these people, any enjoyment they got from watching the cute cat videos was temporary. The shift toward a more positive mood from watching the videos was overshadowed by the guilt they experienced from knowing that they were procrastinating on their important tasks. What they experienced was quite literally a guilty pleasure. They had temporarily traded their negative mood from the task they were avoiding for a fleeting experience of enjoyment while watching the cat videos and an additional boost in negative mood borne out of their own guilt.

In the research we've just discussed, using social media for procrastination was a single or occasional instance. But what happens when procrastination is a more chronic tendency? A group of German researchers set out to answer this question, with some fascinating results (Reinecke et al., 2018). They specifically wanted to examine how and why trait procrastination and internet use was linked to poor mental health, so they surveyed a representative sample of almost 1,600 internet users about their levels of trait procrastination, their psychological health, how often they used the internet, the difficulties they had in controlling their internet use, and whether they believed that their internet use was causing them harm. What they found confirmed the idea that trait procrastination may have cumulative and negative effects on mental health. Not only were people who chronically procrastinated more likely to spend more time on the internet and have difficulty controlling their internet use, but they also believed that their internet use was having harmful effects on other areas of their lives. They knew their internet misuse was bad for them, yet they still couldn't help themselves. The internet was providing them with an emotional escape route to avoid the negative emotions they associated with the things they knew they should be doing.

What about their mental health? Well, as you may have already guessed, people who had high levels of trait procrastination also experienced increased levels of stress, depression, and anxiety. This is not a new revelation. Numerous studies over the past few decades have shown that chronic procrastination is linked to poor psychological health. What this study revealed that had not been shown before, though, is that believing that internet use is harmful is the route by which chronic procrastination affected psychological health. In other words, people who chronically procrastinated experienced poor mental health in part because they knew their excessive internet use was harmful for them.

The findings from this study paint a very different picture of procrastination from what many people envision. Welcome to the world of a chronic procrastinator: It's not filled with fun and games, restorative breaks, or endless hours of guilt-free leisure; instead, guilty pleasures are more guilt laden than pleasurable in the long run, and they take a heavy toll on psychological health.

Take a Moment

Let's pause for a moment. Think about the last time you used social media or the internet as a means of procrastinating. (If you don't do this, congratulations! You've mastered one of life's more pervasive sources of distraction.) Ask yourself: "How aware was I that I was procrastinating while going on my social media channel(s) or the internet?" "How did I feel while I was using my social media or surfing the web?" "How did I feel after I stopped using my social media or the internet?" "Do I believe that being on the internet or my social media channels for too long is unhealthy?"

Why Thinking Too Much About Your Procrastination Can Make Things Worse

Apart from excessive use of the internet, chronic procrastination can lead to vulnerability to poor mental health in other ways. You may have noticed in the internet study we just discussed that people who chronically procrastinated were well aware of how harmful their internet procrastination was for them. They did not appear to be in denial of this. This awareness of how harmful procrastination can be goes hand in hand with not only the guilt and shame people who chronically procrastinate experience but also the thoughts that they have about themselves.

People who are prone to procrastination are also prone to a certain type of negative and repetitive thinking that can amplify their negative mood and create additional vulnerability for poor mental health; specifically, I am referring to rumination. *Rumination* is an automatic, repetitive thinking pattern similar to worry that occurs when a person focuses on their distress and the causes and consequences of this distress. But rather than focusing on solutions to relieve or prevent this distress, people who ruminate get fixated on their emotions. They run the scenarios and possible explanations that led to them feeling distressed over and over in their minds as a way to try and make sense out of what happened. Thoughts such as "Why am I such a loser?" and "Why can't I seem to reach my goals?" predominate the mind of someone who is prone to ruminate. In doing this, though, they reactivate all the negative emotions from the stressful or distressing event that led them to ruminate in the first place.

As you can imagine, if you are constantly and repetitively focusing on the negative thoughts and feelings that come in the wake of procrastination, it isn't going to quiet or resolve them. Instead, ruminating on those negative thoughts will be the equivalent of turning the volume dial of your negative feelings up to the maximum. It comes as no surprise, then, that research has shown that rumination is linked to the development and maintenance of anxiety and depression (McLaughlin & Nolen-Hoeksema, 2011).

What we've been discussing so far describes what happens when people prone to procrastination ruminate about their negative experiences more generally. But what about when we ruminate specifically about our own procrastination? The following example is a good illustration of what this might look like:

> [I arrived] late to my final-ever game as manager for [the] football club who I had managed for 15 years. I simply left everything until the last minute. It meant that I wasn't fully prepared when I arrived, and I then made some rudimentary mistakes because I hadn't given myself the time required for focus because I was still messing around with the little jobs which I could have sorted a lot, lot earlier. It has been a fortnight since this happened and I think about it at least 3 or 4 times a day. I have a huge sense of regret, which also shows itself to me as massive failure. Despite

> all the good things achieved over the previous 15 years, 500-odd
> games and 1,400 training sessions. . . . That last messed-up day
> is the overriding and haunting memory which I cannot shake.
> And it was all avoidable!!

This football manager is haunted by his procrastination in preparing for his final game. Even 2 weeks later he is rehashing the event in his mind three to four times a day, which only fuels his feelings of regret and failure. In addition, his memories of all his past successes are marred by this single act of procrastination. Now, although we don't know exactly what his thoughts were, it is likely that judgments such as "Why did I leave everything to the last minute?" and "I wish I had started preparing earlier" were part of his internal, ruminative dialogue.

Researchers refer to this type of rumination that is focused on past and current procrastination as *procrastinatory cognitions*. Basically, they are repetitive, self-critical thoughts people have when they are feeling bad about their procrastination. Like your garden variety rumination, procrastinatory cognitions focus on trying to make sense of the negative emotions people experience as a means of regaining control over the situation. But these types of thoughts focus on trying to understand the emotional states linked to a failure rather than on actions that might help us avoid the situation in the future. This is why they can leave us feeling overwhelmed and in an even worse negative mood than what we began with. And when these procrastinatory cognitions occur while you are procrastinating, they can be even more harmful by generating additional negative feelings about the task that you are procrastinating. These feelings, in turn, can drive you to procrastinate even further.

As you might have guessed, people who chronically procrastinate are particularly prone to having these procrastinatory cognitions and consequently are at higher risk for distress. Although research on how procrastinatory cognitions are linked to mental health is limited to examining college students, the evidence is quite consistent. One group of researchers found that students with high levels of trait procrastination are more likely to ruminate about their procrastination and in turn experience increased negative mood, stress, distress, and increased procrastination (Flett et al., 2012). Put simply, procrastinatory cognitions feed into a vicious circle of poor mental health and further procrastination, which then feed into each other in reciprocal, mutually reinforcing ways. It's even harder to get motivated to do unpleasant tasks when you're feeling depressed.

Thankfully, though, you can take steps to quiet these repetitive thoughts and break the cycle of rumination and poor mental health. The "Becoming Aware of How Procrastination Affects Your Mental Health" exercise provides examples of some of these science-supported activities. For example, in one study people who took a 90-minute walk in nature experienced lower levels of rumination than those who walked for the same amount of time in an urban setting (Bratman et al., 2015). Also, neural activity in the areas of the brain linked to the development of mental health issues was reduced among the nature walkers.

You may have noticed that we've not really talked much about stress up to this point in our discussion of how procrastination affects mental health. This is not because procrastination isn't linked to stress—quite the contrary. Research has shown consistently that people who procrastinate experience higher levels of stress. My omission of the topic of stress in relation to procrastination was by design. We often think of stress as falling mainly under the umbrella of mental health, but the topic of stress actually straddles the border between mental and physical health (if such a border even exists). Because much of the research on procrastination and stress has focused on their implications for physical health, I have instead decided to include stress in a specific section of this chapter that discusses physical health, our next topic.

> ## EXERCISE: Becoming Aware of How Procrastination Affects Your Mental Health
>
> Becoming aware of when and why you procrastinate is the first step toward finding solutions to getting procrastination under control. But sometimes, if we reflect too much on our procrastination, this can turn into brooding and unhealthy repetitive thinking that can take a toll on mental health. This exercise will guide you through how to recognize and then address your repetitive thoughts about procrastinating.
>
> **Awareness:** What thoughts tend to preoccupy your mind when you are procrastinating? Do you notice any themes that repeat? Write these down.
>
> _____
>
> _____
>
> Do you find it hard to stop or shut down these thoughts once they get started?
>
> ☐ YES   ☐ NO
>
> If you've replied "YES," then you may wish to try some of the strategies below to help you get a better handle on these thoughts and reduce the risk they can pose to your mental health.
>
> If you've replied "NO," that's great news. You may still want to monitor these thoughts for signs of when they may become repetitive.
>
> **Action:** There are a number of science-supported strategies you can use to help get your repetitive thoughts about procrastination under control. Below is a list of some that have been shown to help people manage rumination. Find the ones that work best for you by taking a trial-and-error approach. If one doesn't work for you, don't be discouraged—chances are another might be better suited to your own needs.
>
> 1. **Spend some time in nature.** Research has shown that spending time in nature—in particular, walking—can help reduce rumination. Aim to take a walk for 60 to 90 minutes in a green, nonurban space to get the most benefits.

EXERCISE: Becoming Aware of How Procrastination Affects Your Mental Health (*Continued*)

2. **Meditate.** Engaging in meditative practices such as mindfulness has been shown to be beneficial for quieting ruminative thoughts. A number of smartphone apps and online programs are available that can guide you toward calming your mind and thoughts. With practice over time, meditation can help you feel more in control of your automatic thoughts and avoid rumination.

3. **Exercise.** Engaging in a single session of exercise for 40 to 60 minutes, from walking, to workouts, to ball sports, has been shown to reduce ruminative thinking (and boost mood) in people with mental health issues. The form of the exercise is less important than the time spent exercising. You can even combine exercise with time spent in nature to get added benefits.

I'LL LOOK AFTER MY HEALTH, LATER

When people first hear the idea that procrastination can be bad for their physical health, they often think of all those unused gym memberships and broken diet promises. The evidence certainly supports these conclusions and shows that procrastinating important health behaviors is not only very common but also costly for both our health and our pocketbooks. For example, a survey of more than 400 adults in Israel found that health improvement was the most frequent area of life in which people procrastinated (Hen & Goroshit, 2018).

Consider also that, as mentioned in Chapter 1, within 6 months of starting a gym membership more than 50% of people stop going and that the estimated cost of this procrastination is a whopping $49 million a year. What about healthy eating? The statistics are just as, if not more, appalling. It's estimated that only about 20% of people who start making changes to their diet are actually able to

73

stick with the changes 3 months later. A further 40%, or two out of five people, have abandoned the positive changes to their diet within the first week (*Daily Mail*, 2013). Clearly, problems bridging the intention–behavior gap are rampant when it comes to making health behavior changes.

Putting off intended and important heath behavior changes is certainly one way that procrastination can take a toll on your physical health, but what people often don't realize is that these instances of health procrastination have the potential to add up over time and take a much more serious toll, especially when you factor in the stress associated with procrastination. In this section, I present evidence on some of the surprising health costs of procrastination, including its impact on acute and chronic health problems, putting off seeking medical attention, higher stress, poor coping, poor sleep, and even bedtime procrastination.

But before we start exploring the various costs to physical health procrastination has, let's back up a bit and return to the study that I mentioned at the opening of this chapter. The study that introduced the idea that procrastination may be bad for your health. The study that was the starting point for my own research program about how and why procrastination may affect physical health and the insights I am sharing with you in this chapter.

Back in 1997, researchers Diane Tice and Roy Baumeister conducted a study with college students to see whether a tendency to procrastinate created a risk for stress and poor health (Tice & Baumeister, 1997). They surveyed a small group of students twice, once at the beginning of the semester and once at the end of the semester, right before the final exams. In each survey the students were asked to report their procrastination tendencies (aka *trait procrastination*), their weekly stress and physical symptoms, and the number of visits they had made to the college health care center in the past month.

The results were surprising: The students who had a strong tendency to procrastinate reported less stress and fewer illness symptoms at the beginning of the term. In contrast, their nonprocrastinating counterparts appeared to be worse off; they reported higher stress and more physical symptoms of illness as the term got underway. But if we fast forward to the end-of-term exam period and when assignments were due, who do you think was suffering more now? If you guessed that the procrastinators were now more stressed and physically ill, you're right. Although procrastinating appeared to serve a protective function in regard to illness and stress at the beginning of the term, it became a vulnerability by the end of term as the deadlines for assignments and studying for exams loomed.

As intriguing as the results from this study were, they raised a few questions for me that begged further investigation. If you recall from Chapter 2, students who procrastinate are also prone to making bogus excuses to get extensions on the work they have procrastinated on. So, how did we know that the trips to the health center were genuinely linked to poor health and not just a way to fake a medical reason for an extension? Tice and Baumeister speculated that the higher stress that students experienced was responsible for their poor physical health, but they didn't actually test this in their study. Last, procrastination is rampant among college students, perhaps because of the numerous deadlines they face on a regular basis. How do we know that the effects on physical health found in this study apply to other people who are not students?

These burning questions led me to not only conduct a number of studies over the years to try and find the answers but also to develop conceptual models to better explain why and how procrastination might make people more vulnerable to poor physical health. I'm not going to go into all of this research here; instead, I want to highlight some of the key findings from my own research, and that of others, that both illustrate and explain the consequences of procrastination for your physical health.

From Stress to Poor Health Behaviors, Procrastination Isn't Healthy

Beyond addressing the main focus of this chapter—the costs to health of procrastination—I also believe that understanding the range of ways that procrastination can affect your physical health is important because it helps you recognize how procrastination, especially chronic procrastination, may be affecting your life. To this end, I've created an exercise, which appears at the end of this chapter ("Becoming Aware of How Procrastination Affects Your Physical Health"), to help you map the different ways that procrastination may be influencing your health. Again, the aim is not to make you feel guilty but to instead help you have some compassion for yourself and the difficulties that procrastination may be causing you. If you saw that a good friend was experiencing poor health because of their procrastinating, wouldn't you want to help them by being supportive and compassionate?

Let's start with the questions of how and why procrastination may be bad for your health. As we will see, these two questions are closely linked. Because chronic procrastination is a behavioral tendency that is akin to a personality trait, it makes sense to use insights from personality science to guide this research. We know, for example, that personality traits can affect health, for better or worse, through two key routes: (a) stress and (b) health behaviors.

Traits that put people in situations that are both stressful and negatively affect how they cope with that stress, can make them vulnerable to poor health. The harmful effects of acute bouts of stress for health are well documented and can range from headaches, to minor digestive issues, even a compromised immune system. Think about the last time you went through a stressful period. It's likely that soon after the situation passed you found yourself sick with a cold or flu bug. Why? Because the stress weakened your immune system and made it less able to fight off the numerous bugs and viruses that we are all exposed to each day, which then made it easier for you to become ill.

People's personality traits can also increase their risk for poor physical health because they predispose them to certain unhealthy habits and ways of behaving. For example, unhealthy traits that interfere with self-regulation also make it difficult to engage in the behaviors that maintain and promote good physical health. Recall from Chapter 1 that self-regulation reflects the psychological processes involved in managing our thoughts, feelings, and behaviors. When we have good self-regulation skills we are also able to set, monitor, and reach our health goals and take action to close the gap between our intentions and our behavior.

It's not surprising that decades of research have established that engaging in healthy behaviors such as eating a nutritious diet and maintaining an appropriate weight, staying physically active, and getting sufficient sleep are essential for good health. Most of us know that not practicing these good habits will likely have both short- and long-term negative consequences for our physical health. Poor eating and sleep habits can jointly be harmful for your physical health. Add to this a dash of being sedentary more often than not, and you have a good recipe for being more likely to experience a number of physical health issues in the short term. If you fast forward to the future, you will realize that the cumulative effects of these poor health behaviors on your physical well-being can be even more concerning. Over time, the risk of obesity significantly increases, as does the risk of developing of a number of chronic diseases, such as diabetes, heart disease, arthritis, even cancer.

It should be fairly clear at this point that chronic procrastination fits the profile of an unhealthy trait. From the perspective of personality science, it makes sense, then, that higher stress and poor health behaviors explain why people who procrastinate regularly often experience poorer physical health. This is the logic that has guided much of the research I have conducted over the past two decades on the impact of procrastination on health. And the evidence from this research supports this view of how procrastination affects health. In Chapter 5, we delve more into the reasons why this is the case as we explore the psychological processes that underpin procrastination. For now, though, research has consistently shown that people who chronically procrastinate tend to have higher levels of stress and engage in fewer healthy behaviors.

For example, Tim Pychyl and I conducted a study with undergraduate students at three points in the academic term to see how trait procrastination was linked to their stress, health, behavior, and physical health problems (Sirois & Pychyl, 2002). We basically wanted to replicate and extend what that initial study of procrastination and health had found. Instead of a small group of students, we had almost 400 students complete our surveys. At all three points in the term we found that students who were chronic procrastinators reported higher levels of stress; less frequent practice of health-promoting behaviors, such as regular exercise and healthy eating; and a greater number of stress-related health problems, such as colds and flus, headaches, and muscle tension.

We also examined whether the higher stress and fewer healthy behaviors reported by the student procrastinators explained their poor physical health. It turned out that stress, but not poor health behaviors, accounted in part for the greater number of health problems that these students experienced. Now, perhaps these students' relative youth and good health made them resilient to the costs of having poor health habits. It's quite possible that, over time, the consequences of eating too much fast food, skipping meals, and being a couch potato will affect the students' physical health.

As it turns out, this does in fact appear to be the case. Over the years, I've conducted a number of studies on how procrastination affects health with adults who were not students, and even with nurses, who you would expect to know better when it comes to health-related matters. In each of these studies people who were prone to procrastination reported experiencing higher stress, practicing fewer health-promoting behaviors, and having more physical ailments. But, for these adults, many of whom were middle aged, procrastinating on important health behaviors, such as healthy eating and having an active lifestyle, did explain, in part, why they had a poorer state of physical health. So, although the undergrad students may be immune to the immediate impact of procrastinating on eating healthily and exercising regularly, other adults may not be. In short, people who are not students and who chronically procrastinate may be at even greater risk for poor health than students.

I'll Visit the Doctor, Later

Up to this point we've mainly focused on how chronic procrastination can take a toll on health by impeding the practice of health-promoting behaviors such as healthy eating and physical activity. But these aren't the only types of health-related behaviors that people who are prone to procrastinate struggle with. In fact, research has demonstrated that there is a range of behaviors essential to maintaining good health and preventing disease that are compromised when we chronically procrastinate. Figure 3.1 gives a visual overview of these behaviors.

If you're prone to procrastinate on one type of health behavior, it's not much of a stretch to imagine how this may make it easier to procrastinate other behaviors that are important for health as well. Seeking medical attention when needed is one example. I've consistently found in my research that people who chronically

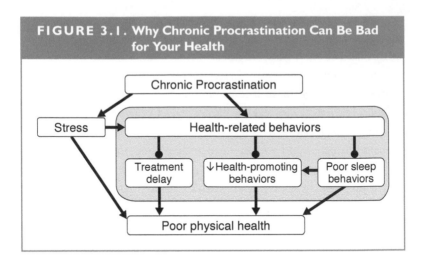

FIGURE 3.1. Why Chronic Procrastination Can Be Bad for Your Health

procrastinate also tend to delay seeking medical and dental care until it is absolutely necessary.

Apart from delaying seeking dental care, which is something many people find unpleasant, it seems counterintuitive that you would put off getting medical attention that would have the potential to give you relief from the discomfort of troubling physical symptoms. Avoiding unpleasant feelings and experiences is what drives procrastination, after all. But if we consider that troubling physical symptoms can also bring to mind worries about more serious diagnoses that are lurking beneath those symptoms, then it makes some sense why someone might delay seeing their doctor. The problem is that such delays can result in a health issue that has become worse, or more advanced, because it wasn't treated in time. The following passage is just one of many stories I have heard from people who put off getting the medical care they needed because they struggled with procrastination:

> I procrastinated in going to the hospital when I didn't feel well. I procrastinated for 3 weeks and the health issue was very serious. I spent 1 week in hospital. I felt tired, discouraged, and disappointed that I didn't take better care of myself and be kind to my body.

Although this person did eventually seek the care they needed, they still felt bad about the delay and for not having taken care of themselves. They experienced the same types of negative feelings and regret that tend to follow any type of procrastination.

I'll Get a Good Night's Sleep, Later

Procrastination can also compromise our sleep. Imagine that you have a report due in the next couple of days for work that you've been putting off. A lot is riding on this report both for yourself and for your company. How easy do you think it would be to get a good night's sleep with all the stress from this looming deadline? And if you decided to pull an all-nighter and did manage to get it done in time, what would the aftereffects be for your sleep schedule?

Not surprisingly, when my colleagues and I surveyed Canadian and Greek undergraduate students about their procrastination tendencies and sleep habits, we found that those who were prone to procrastinating reported that they had a poorer quality of sleep (Sirois et al., 2015). They slept for fewer hours each night. They felt unrested when they woke and had trouble staying awake during the day. They needed medication to help them sleep. These student procrastinators also experienced high levels of stress, and this stress made it difficult for them to get a good night's sleep.

Procrastination can compromise our sleep in other ways as well. Consider, for example, when we put off going to bed at a reasonable hour or at the time we intended to. Let's say you've got an important meeting the next morning at 9:00 and need to get to bed by 11:00 p.m. to feel rested and alert, but instead you end up staying up until 2:00 a.m. because you were binge-watching funny cat videos and lost track of time.

Researchers refer to this particular type of procrastination as *bedtime procrastination* because it involves putting off going to bed when you intended to, without any good reason, yet knowing that you will be worse off for doing so. Unfortunately, bedtime procrastination is all too common. Research from the United States and the Netherlands suggests that about 50% of people admit to bedtime procrastinating once or more in any given week (Kroese et al., 2016).

If we consider the consequences of not getting enough good quality sleep for our health, then the implications of procrastination for sleep are very concerning. Not getting enough sleep each night over as short a period as 1 week is known to compromise the immune system's capacity to fight off infections and viruses. When we don't get enough sleep our bodies release more of the stress hormone cortisol, which makes us more reactive to minor challenges and less resilient to stress. Lack of sleep can also interfere with staying on track with your health goals. It's much harder to stick to your workout routine when you are tired. Plus, your sleep-starved brain finds it harder to exercise control over your eating impulses and resist temptations than when you are well rested. This means that you are more susceptible to cravings for unhealthy high-carb and high-fat snacks (i.e., junk food), late night eating, and eating larger portions of food than you need. In short, not getting enough sleep can derail your best intentions to stick to a healthy diet.

What Happens to Your Health When You Chronically Procrastinate?

In addition to the examples just given, stress can interfere with our intentions to follow through with a number of behaviors that are important for staying healthy. From dieting and exercise, to seeking medical care and following medical regimens, to getting a good night's sleep, the stress from procrastinating can amplify the other harmful effects of procrastination on your health. Moreover, over time high levels of stress and poor health behaviors are well known to have a synergistic and cumulative effect that can increase risk for a number of serious and chronic health conditions. If procrastinating has become a chronic tendency, along with a general pattern of chronic stress and neglect of important health behaviors, then it's not hard to imagine that the impact of procrastination on your health over years or decades will not be a positive one.

This is not just a speculation. To test these ideas, I conducted a study of almost 1,000 people to see whether chronic procrastination was linked to poor heart health (Sirois, 2015). I compared a group of people who reported that they had high blood pressure, heart disease, or both with another group who were free from any type of chronic illness. I also accounted for a number of other factors that might contribute to risk for poor heart health in my analysis, such as age, gender, and education level, as well as other personality traits known to affect heart health.

The results were alarming, even to me. Not only did the people with poor heart health report higher levels of chronic procrastination, but for every 1-point increase on a 5-point measure of chronic procrastination the chances of them being in the group of people with poor heart health increased by an astounding 63%. Now, these results aren't conclusive. The people in the study were surveyed at only a single time point, not over time, and other factors were not taken into account, so we can't be sure of the extent to which chronic procrastination may have contributed to developing poor heart health in light of other risk factors, such as family history and other stressors. But because stress, poor health behaviors, and poor sleep are all well-established risk factors for high blood pressure and heart disease, this study provides some suggestive and alarming evidence that chronic procrastination may be a risk factor for having poor heart health.

Instead of ending this chapter on a sobering note, this is a good place to remind you of why it is important to understand the full scope of the consequences procrastination has for physical and mental health. Yes, the research tells a pretty grim story about what happens to our mental and physical health when we procrastinate, especially when our procrastination tendencies become chronic. But that is only one side of the story.

We can flip these results around to also tell a story of the benefits that we can reap when we start to understand and reduce our own procrastination. For example, in the study I just described, if you decreased your tendency to procrastinate by 1 point, this could mean that you could potentially reduce your risk for poor heart health by 63%. The good news is that when we reduce our tendencies to procrastinate, we can expect to have better mental health, a lower risk for illness and physical health problems, lower stress levels, and better sleep, as well as being better able to take care of ourselves.

EXERCISE: Becoming Aware of How Procrastination Affects Your Physical Health

Whether or not procrastination is chronic or occasional, research supports the idea that procrastination can be bad for your health, but sometimes we are not always aware of the extent to which our own procrastination can affect our health. The questions below are a starting point to raise your awareness about these consequences. The intent is not to make you feel bad about these impacts, but simply to increase your awareness of them. Remember that research indicates that health is one of the most common areas of life where people procrastinate. You are not alone. Many of us have the best of intentions when it comes to improving our health but struggle to put those intentions into action. Identifying areas of your health that might be taking a hit from procrastination can be a first step toward taking counteractive measures to reduce procrastination so you can be healthier and achieve your health goals.

Has procrastination increased your stress levels?

1	2	3	4	5	6	7	8	9	10

No, not at all   **Somewhat**   **Yes, quite a bit**

Have your health behaviors been affected by your procrastination?

1	2	3	4	5	6	7	8	9	10

No, not at all   **Somewhat**   **Yes, quite a bit**

Has procrastination affected your health?

1	2	3	4	5	6	7	8	9	10

No, not at all   **Somewhat**   **Yes, quite a bit**

Have you put off going to the doctor when you know you should have?

1	2	3	4	5	6	7	8	9	10

No, not at all   **Somewhat**   **Yes, quite a bit**

CHAPTER 4

PROCRASTINATION THROUGH A SOCIAL LENS

Even when we do wrong, accountability is helpful, compassion is helpful, apology and forgiveness are helpful, but shame is not.
—Debra Campbell

In this chapter, you will learn

- how procrastination can affect your personal and professional relationships,
- how other people view procrastinators and how this can affect the way you view your own procrastination, and
- how to break the cycle of guilt and shame linked to procrastination.

When we think about the costs of procrastination, it's easy to just focus on the costs to ourselves. Putting things off unnecessarily can mean that we are less productive. It can mean that we don't reach our personal goals. As we saw in the last chapter, procrastination can also mean that our physical and mental health take a hit. But procrastination doesn't happen in a vacuum. We exist in a social world where our lives, goals, and dreams are intertwined with those of others. When we unnecessarily delay important tasks in our work and personal lives, we inevitably affect the lives of those around us.

In this chapter, we explore some of the ways that procrastination can influence our social relationships. Although there is relatively less research on this topic, the evidence suggests that our procrastination can have some very real impacts on the people in our lives.

It's important to be aware of these social costs, for a number of reasons. Although we may not always be aware of the actual consequences for others, our procrastination can have a variety of effects that result in inconvenience, losses, or even stress. These consequences are usually not what we would wish on anyone or knowingly set in motion. Becoming more aware of these costs can make it less easy to slip into complacency about our procrastination. It becomes harder to resign ourselves to just live with it. As we discuss shortly, these social costs can also have cumulative effects that may come back to haunt us, especially if our procrastination is a more regular habit. In short, when our procrastination has a negative impact on others, this usually also will affect us.

CONSEQUENCES FOR FRIENDS AND FAMILY

When we unnecessarily put off important tasks that involve others, the social consequences are often quite clear. Consider the following example, from a person who put off planning a social event, resulting in a lost opportunity to connect with a friend: "[I] put off contacting a friend to arrange a social occasion and it ended up not happening." The loss here is for both parties. The friend quite likely had been looking forward to the get-together and may have been disappointed that it was never arranged. But the person who put off setting up the social occasion lost out as well. What about when a procrastinated social event is more meaningful, such as a birthday or meeting a friend or family member who was in town only for a short time? In these circumstances, the cost of social procrastination is even higher.

Sometimes when we procrastinate on important tasks that are relevant for other people, the costs can have consequences that are not immediately clear to us. We may anticipate only the future consequences to our family:

When both of my children were born I had every intention of keeping a "baby book" for each of them. My mother had kept very detailed notes about my first years in a baby book, and I wanted to do the same for my children. I had books purchased, but never opened them. Days would pass and every day I would mentally say, "You HAVE to do this, you will regret it otherwise." My boys are now 6 and 3, and I never did complete their baby books. Already, I am forgetting special memories and dates like first words and first steps. I have now procrastinated to a point where starting the project would almost be impossible. I don't have the details to write in the books. I am angry with myself that my boys will not have any information on the "firsts" in their life. Honestly, I feel like I have failed their "future selves."

In this example, the mother is overwhelmed by regret from her procrastination because of how she believes it will affect her children in the future. Note that she was well aware that she would experience regret from procrastinating, but that wasn't enough to prompt her to action. Although it's difficult to estimate how much her children will be affected by her lack of action, she will nonetheless likely carry this regret for some time to come.

This is where the real cost of procrastination can come into play. It's quite likely that her boys will not miss that they don't have their "firsts" recorded somewhere. They will not be expecting the detailed notes that their grandmother had kept for their mother and that their mother in turn wished she had kept for them. You can't be disappointed by not getting something you never expected. Ignorance is bliss, as they say. But what her boys will more likely experience is their mother's lingering regret over procrastinating on preparing her sons' baby books. Whether she voices it or not, their mother's regret may loom over and cloud other happy moments they share. Regret is an emotion tied to the past, to "should-haves" and "could-haves." Focusing on regret may take her out of those moments of being truly present with her boys and making new memories, shifting her focus instead to the past as she is haunted by the ghosts of her procrastination.

If you are starting to feel some compassion for the mother in this example, that's a good thing. She is clearly suffering. When we look at the thoughts that are running through her head, we can understand why she feels so guilty. If, on the other hand, your inner critic is starting to judge her lack of timely action, that's understandable, too: It's a sign that you've embraced the social rules about the importance of following through with our intentions.

When we become too embroiled in our own negative narratives about how shameful and reprimandable our procrastination is, we can not only lose sight of the real ways that our procrastination affects the people in our lives, but we also feed back into the emotional dynamic that led us to procrastinate in the first place. We delve more into how and why these narratives develop in the last section of this chapter.

CONSEQUENCES FOR PEOPLE IN THE WORKPLACE

Chapter 2 highlighted the costs of workplace procrastination, including those to others. From lost productivity, to the technical costs of cyberslacking, procrastinating at work has very real and significant financial costs for employers. But can our procrastination at work affect our fellow employees as well?

There are few work environments where we don't come into contact with others. Whether working in large teams with coworkers, in partnerships in small business, or being self-employed and answering to clients and customers, how productive we are and whether we meet deadlines will inevitably have an impact on other people. When we procrastinate on important work tasks it means we leave our coworkers with less time to make their contributions and fulfill their work responsibilities. This can put time pressure on them and create unnecessary stress. When we don't follow through and complete tasks that others may be waiting for, we essentially end up not honoring our commitments. This can affect both how others view us and how we view ourselves.

What Happens When Coworkers Procrastinate?

So how do people view coworkers who procrastinate? My colleague Wendelien van Eerde, from the Business School at the University of Amsterdam, and I conducted a study to answer exactly this question (van Eerde & Sirois, 2021). We instructed a group of about 100 employees to imagine that a new coworker, Robin, would be joining their team to work on a new project that had tight deadlines. We also told them that the project was complex and required dedication and good cooperation from everyone to be successful.

We then asked the employees to read one of three different descriptions of Robin. In the first description, Robin was described as someone who procrastinates frequently; delays work tasks; almost always doesn't follow through with what they say they will do; fails to meet deadlines; and is always making promises that are not kept, despite knowing there will be negative consequences. In the second description Robin was presented as a moderate procrastinator, who sometimes fails to meet deadlines, and so on, and in the last description Robin was portrayed as someone who keeps their promises, completes work on time, and rarely delays work. After reading the description of Robin, we asked the employees to rate how likable and dependable they thought Robin was. We also asked them how much they would want to work with Robin.

Much to our surprise, Robin was viewed as equally likable regardless of how much they procrastinated. Basically, Robin was seen as being a nice person whether described as someone who put things off a lot and caused problems for others or as someone who promptly took care of tasks at work. However, the employees' opinion of Robin's dependability did rely on whether Robin procrastinated. When Robin was described as an extreme or even moderate procrastinator, the employees rated Robin as being less dependable than the nonprocrastinating version. When Robin was described as someone who procrastinated frequently or occasionally, they also rated Robin as someone with whom they would not enjoy working. The take-home message here is that people might think that coworkers who procrastinate are nice people but just not very dependable, nor someone with whom they really would want to work, especially on important projects.

One of the striking things about procrastination at work is the way that it can affect our relationships with coworkers. Sure, we may still be thought of as nice or even fun, but when push comes to shove, if procrastination becomes an all-too-familiar habit then people may shy away from wanting to work with us when given a choice. And if they don't have a choice, then they may feel frustrated by the restraints that your procrastination puts on their own work goals and aspirations.

What Happens When Leaders Procrastinate?

In the research study I just described, the new employee who was a procrastinator was presented as a coworker who answered to the same supervisor or manager as the employees we studied. But what happens when the person who is procrastinating is a leader rather than a coworker? Researchers from the United Kingdom and Australia conducted two studies with employees and their supervisors to address this question (Legood et al., 2018). The results of the first study indicated that employees viewed managers who procrastinated and delayed making decisions until it was too late as being less effective leaders. Perceiving our leaders as being less effective can erode our trust in them and their decisions. This can then translate into less willingness to engage with our work and result in poor productivity. If your manager isn't following through with what she or he said, and procrastinating, then it's easier for you to do the same.

However, this wasn't the only way that leaders who procrastinated affected their employees. In the second study, the researchers followed teams of supervisors and their employees over a 3-week period. They asked employees to rate their levels of frustration with their work and supervisors to rate their employees' behavior; specifically, they asked supervisors whether their employees displayed any signs of good organizational citizenship, such as helping others at work. They also asked supervisors whether their employees showed signs of poor work engagement, for example, by calling in sick when they weren't really ill.

What they found was a very interesting yet disruptive dynamic between the supervisors and their employees. Supervisors who were viewed as being procrastinators by their employees in turn reported that their employees were more likely to engage in deviant work behaviors that negatively affected their productivity. They also viewed their employees as not being particularly good organizational citizens.

What about the employees? Well, not surprisingly, employees who worked under supervisors with a leadership style fraught with procrastination reported high levels of frustration with not being able to get their jobs done. This makes some sense if we consider that supervisors are often gatekeepers for resources and information that employees need to fulfill their job responsibilities. If employees are blocked from accessing the resources they need to reach their work goals because their supervisors have delayed replying to requests or making decisions, then frustration is a natural and understandable response.

Taken together, these studies tell us that procrastination at work can erode our work relationships. It can turn from being simply self-defeating, by negatively affecting our reputation, to being other-defeating, by having a detrimental impact on the work habits and productivity of others.

Now, there may be times when our apparent procrastination is unintentional. In this case, it really isn't procrastination at all but some other form of delay. I say "apparent" because many people confuse rational or meaningful delay for procrastination. On the surface, the two appear to be the same. People observe that an important work task has been delayed or not completed, perhaps because a supervisor has delayed making a decision or replying to an employee because they were waiting to receive essential information before doing so—a classic example of sagacious delay. But without knowing the complete story as to *why* there was a delay, some people may simply assume that their supervisor was procrastinating. If they do, then the consequences, as we've just seen, can be detrimental for everyone.

This highlights the importance of communication between leaders and their subordinates in the work environment. If leaders are clear and proactive about why they are delaying decisions and providing resources and feedback, then this can minimize the appearance of procrastination when in fact they are simply delaying for good reasons. After all, as we will see shortly, procrastination is viewed much more negatively than is a justified delay. Good communication from leaders can, in turn, lessen the negative impact of such delays on their employees and improve the organizational culture. As I outline toward the end of this chapter, communicating and being up front with others is always a good strategy, especially when our delay is an instance of true procrastination.

WHAT DO OTHER PEOPLE THINK OF PROCRASTINATORS?

By this point in the chapter, it should be clear to you that people can hold negative views about those who procrastinate. In the work environment, for example, people who procrastinate are judged as being undependable and as someone who might interfere with your capacity to reach your work goals. These perceptions may be enough reason for you to decide to avoid working with them altogether. What's interesting, though, is that these judgments about procrastinators often are made automatically, without any interaction with that person. The label "procrastinator" carries negative connotations that can shape our views of others and, for that matter, ourselves.

So, where do these negative views of procrastination come from? We could guess that they come from our past experiences of interacting with someone who procrastinated and experiencing subsequent problems. Or if we have not ever dealt with anyone who procrastinated, then we could have heard from other people who had bad experiences with a coworker or friend who procrastinated. In short, it is likely that our views of people who procrastinate as having undesirable qualities are due to beliefs that we acquire through our direct and indirect social contact with others. We call this *social learning*.

Take a Moment

Let's pause here. Ask yourself: "What qualities come to mind when I think about someone who is a procrastinator?" "How would I describe this person to other people who didn't know them?" "Do I think of that person in negative terms or positive terms?" "Where did these judgments come from?"

Why Procrastination Means Breaking Social Norms

Social norms are the rules that we learn not only through our interactions with others but also through what we hear from others about whether a certain behavior is acceptable. Social norms evolve to help people interact with each other in fair and equitable ways. Once we learn the social norms for how to behave, they operate somewhat automatically. This allows us to make quick decisions about what we should and should not do as well as what we expect others should and shouldn't be doing. In short, social norms facilitate healthy social functioning.

For example, being able to self-regulate your behavior by following through on actions you promised to do, and completing intended tasks and goals, are actions that contribute to a well-functioning social group and to society. Meeting our goals can contribute not only to our own success but also to the success of the smaller and larger social groups to which we belong. When we finish our home renovations instead of procrastinating them, it benefits our family. When we reach our academic goals and educate ourselves, we increase our chances of making a contribution to improve society. When we fulfill our promises to others to complete things, it signals that we are reliable and can be counted on. In other words, social norms set an expectation that we should succeed at regulating our behaviors for the benefit of everyone. When we fail at self-regulation and procrastinate, we transgress these social norms.

The reactions we have to someone who has contravened a social norm is usually swift and automatic. After all, social norms are mental shortcuts to help us navigate the world. So, when we encounter or hear about someone who breaks a social norm, we unfortunately will devalue that person and ascribe a variety of undesirable qualities to them on the basis of their antinormative behavior. For example, when someone procrastinates it sends the message that this person has a number of less-than-flattering qualities, such as being lazy, not managing time well, being impulsive, and being inconsiderate of others. This is why the procrastinating versions of Robin, the hypothetical employee in the research study discussed earlier, were viewed as not being dependable. Robin's behavior transgressed social norms and signaled that they would not be likely to fulfill their obligations and commitments.

When we are the person who is procrastinating, the same social norms are activated. The automatic judgments that we tend to make when we learn about someone else procrastinating are also in triggered when we are the one who isn't following through with our intended actions. And if these norms lead us to make these negative judgments about other people who procrastinate, then it's reasonable to expect that other people will also be likely to make those same judgments about us. Consider, for example, the following situation, in which someone procrastinated at work:

> Felt like I did it again, procrastinating a task due the next day. My breath was short, my heart raced. I felt ashamed about taking so long to do something so simple. Felt I was cheating my team who relied on me for this particular task. Felt I was going to be perceived as unprofessional, unreliable, unknowledgeable. Felt like a failure for not gathering all the required information required to make the event an utmost success. Still managed to leave something [to] the very very last minute and expected to be able to "wing" it.

This person was clearly aware of the potential negative impact of procrastinating on their team, but they were also acutely aware how others might view them for procrastinating—as someone who was unreliable, unprofessional, and unknowledgeable. Now, whether their team would actually view them that way is hard to say. And really, it's less important than the fact that this person *believed* that they would be perceived this way. Just thinking that others will devalue them because of their procrastination was distressing and made them feel like a failure.

Breaking Social Norms Gives Rise to Shame and Guilt

This is one reason why we typically feel bad when we procrastinate. We know we have transgressed a social norm about how to behave. And when we go against social norms, we experience negative social emotions in the form of guilt or shame. This is why in the example just given, and in many other examples throughout this book, you will read of people mentioning that they felt ashamed and guilty about their procrastination. It's a natural emotional response that we have when we have transgressed a social norm.

Now, although both guilt and shame have their genesis in the breaking of social norms, they are distinct in a couple of important ways. *Guilt* results when we perceive that the cause of transgressing a social norm is our behavior: Put simply, we experience guilt when we believe that we did something bad. *Shame*, on the other hand, results when we go beyond our norm-transgressing behavior to make a judgment about the underlying cause of that behavior, namely our character. We experience shame when we conclude that the reason we acted badly was because we are a bad person and that, because of our behavior, others will come to this same conclusion.

Because behavior can be changed, guilt in most instances can be a powerful motivator to not repeat the same mistakes so that we don't end up violating norms in the future. In this way guilt can be functional—it's a means to an end. This is why making people feel guilty is often promoted as a way of helping them improve themselves and making amends for any harms caused by their behavior. Unfortunately for someone who is prone to procrastination, *any* negative feelings linked to their behavior are more likely to perpetuate rather than correct their behavior. We explore the psychological dynamics of how this works in more detail in Chapter 5.

In regard to shame, things are less straightforward. Changing who we are and our way of being is usually not something that can be easily done, so when we experience feelings of shame due to our procrastination, we may view ourselves as unworthy or defective because we didn't follow through with our intentions. This most often leads to a desire to withdraw and avoid others out of a fear of rejection. So now, on top of wanting to avoid the unpleasant task that prompted us to procrastinate in the first place, we also want to avoid anyone who depends on us to finish that task and will be affected by our unnecessary delay.

In essence, shame adds another layer of avoidance onto the avoidance we are already engaged in when we procrastinate. Recall from Chapter 2 that students who procrastinate often use bogus excuses and fake medical letters to cover up their procrastination. The students are likely using these morally questionable behaviors as a means to cope with the shame they felt when they anticipated that their procrastination would be revealed.

BREAKING THE CYCLE OF GUILT AND SHAME

Whether we like to admit it or not, the people in our lives are an integral part of the narrative of our procrastination. The stories of our lost opportunities, failed goals, and missed shared experiences are interwoven with, and inform, the stories of the relationships they have with us, yet their stories are rarely as judgmental of us as we may anticipate them to be. In fact, it's most often us, rather than others, who hold harshly negative views of our procrastination. We are the ones who judge ourselves as being unworthy, flawed, and a failure, and because we know that procrastination means we have broken social norms, we expect others to view us the same way. As I noted earlier, the feelings of guilt and shame we experience when we transgress social norms can feed into further procrastination and avoidance and even more guilt and shame.

How can we break free from this cycle of guilt and shame? Well, the simple answer is to reach out for help and understanding from the people in our lives. We could approach the people whom our procrastination may have affected and be honest and willing to be held accountable for our actions. We can be up front about why we procrastinated. We could also ask others for assistance if the reason for our unnecessary delay is because we lack confidence or time or resources necessary to complete our task. Sounds easy, right? Well, not quite.

When we are operating from a position of guilt and shame about our procrastination we know at some unconscious level that we went against social norms. Our first inclination will then be to not draw attention to our procrastination. We will want to hide it, or even make excuses for it by blaming outside causes. Being up front about your procrastination or seeking support would be like waving a red flag to say, "Look at me, I've procrastinated!" However, decades of research have clearly shown that when we reach out to others for support when we are struggling, this can help reduce our stress and make it easier to solve the problems with which we are struggling. When we request and accept support from others it can also strengthen our social bonds with the people in our lives.

Aside from drawing attention to your procrastination, reaching out to others for support can also be difficult because you may not feel that you deserve help. After all, shame is linked to feelings of being unworthy. Your first instinct may be that others will reject your requests for help and that they will have a "You made your bed, you lie in it" attitude to your procrastination.

In research conducted by me and one of my doctoral students, this is exactly what we found (Sirois & Yang, 2021). In two separate studies, one with about 200 adults from the community, and another with about 600 nurses, people who were more prone to procrastination were less likely to perceive that they had the support of others. Note that this is "perceived" social support. The support could very well have been available to them, free for the asking, so to speak. But because those prone to procrastination believed that they did not have the support of others, they were less likely to ask for help.

There are other hurdles we have to deal with before we can be up-front about our procrastination. We may have to swallow our pride about appearing "perfect" if we want to be honest with others. As we see in Chapter 6, this can be quite difficult if you are prone to procrastination, yet it is important to remember just how common procrastination is. Reminding yourself that you are not the first person to procrastinate, nor will you be the last, can help address the pride that may be holding you back from being up front with others.

When you are honest about your procrastination and reach out for help, you show other people that you are not perfect but simply human. Rather than engendering criticism, this approach is more likely to earn their respect for being honest and accountable. Most societies place a high value on honesty and accountability because these are two qualities that align with social norms.

By being up-front about your procrastination you may even help other people feel more comfortable and less ashamed about their own procrastination. Your up-front approach will remind them that they aren't the only one who procrastinates, as well as demonstrate a positive way to move past procrastination, guilt, and shame. Between diffusing your feelings of guilt and shame and getting support from others, this approach can make it easier to get back on track, complete your task, and mend any harms to others caused by procrastination. To get started, try working your way through the questions in the "Understanding Postprocrastination Guilt and Shame" exercise.

EXERCISE: Understanding Postprocrastination Guilt and Shame

Recall that both guilt and shame are social emotions that can be triggered when we transgress social norms, such as when we procrastinate. Guilt and shame are closely linked. We experience guilt when we feel we did something wrong, and so we think of that as "bad behavior." But when we infer that the reason we did something wrong is because we are a "bad person," we feel shame. The questions on the audit checklists below will help you get a better understanding of your own feelings of guilt and shame after procrastinating and guide you to see yourself and your behavior in ways that can help you feel less guilty and ashamed after you procrastinate.

Recall a recent time when your procrastination had consequences for other people. Now answer the following questions as honestly as you can. If you find that you are struggling to answer them and starting to feel uncomfortable, remind yourself that you are not the first person to have procrastinated, and you certainly won't be the last.

Guilt Audit

1. What did you procrastinate?
2. Who did your procrastination affect?
3. How do you think it affected them?
4. How did it *actually* affect them? If you are not sure, then note this.
5. What do you think would happen if you were up front with this person about your procrastination? Try to take a balanced perspective and consider possible positives as well.

Shame Audit

1. What are you worried that your procrastination says about you as a person?
2. How do you think others will see you if they knew about your procrastination?
3. Now recall up to three times that you did things that conflict with these views of yourself; for example, if you are worried that you will be seen as being unreliable, think of times when you acted in a dependable and responsible manner.

II

WHEN AND WHY DO PEOPLE PROCRASTINATE?

CHAPTER 5

PROCRASTINATION DECODED: WHY MOOD MATTERS

When awareness is brought to an emotion, power is brought to your life.

—Tara Meyer Robson

In this chapter, you will learn

- why understanding and managing emotions are the key to addressing procrastination,
- how stress can change how we think about time,
- why feeling emotionally connected to your Future Self can be challenging, and
- how to correct temporal shortsightedness and be a better friend to your Future Self.

If you skim through the popular press or productivity blogs to search for ways to tackle procrastination, it won't be long before you come across advice that focuses on how to fix the "causes" of procrastination. Bolster your willpower, curb your impulses to indulge in pleasurable pursuits, manage your time better, or simply dial up your motivation, and you'll be on your way to living a productive and happy procrastination-free life! The unfortunate message embedded within some of this pop culture advice is that people who procrastinate have low willpower, poor impulse control, and lack motivation—in other words, they are lazy and self-indulgent. That's not exactly encouraging or uplifting. And if procrastination has become more than an occasional problem for you, then the judgments implied in this advice are more likely to drive you further toward procrastination than to help you resolve it.

These so-called causes of procrastination can be viewed as a by-product of our deeply rooted social norms about what it means to *not* be productive and contribute to society. As we discovered in Chapter 4, procrastination is viewed in many cultures as a norm-transgressing behavior. It conflicts with the values we hold about thinking of others' well-being, reciprocating help from others, and contributing to society as a whole. Thus, when we procrastinate, we judge ourselves harshly, and we believe that others will also do so because we have acted in way that goes against the expectations that others and society have for us.

If we want to really understand when and why people procrastinate, we need to strip back our negative stereotypes of procrastinators and take a closer look at what's going on beneath the surface of the apparent laziness and lack of motivation. We need to push aside our often-harsh judgments of others and ourselves, and exercise some compassion, to more clearly understand why procrastination has become a way to deal with tasks. We also need to take a more scientific approach to understanding the psychological dynamics involved in procrastination.

When we procrastinate, we sacrifice making progress toward an important, often long-term goal that could have wide-reaching and beneficial effects for both ourselves and others. We also incur costs to ourselves and others in terms of health, well-being, productivity, social trust, and lost opportunities. In effect, we trade the future for the present. The goal also doesn't have to be a big one— even the smallest of goals, if executed in a timely manner, can have a ripple effect in terms of the ultimate downstream benefits.

On the surface, making such a trade-off is irrational. Common sense tells us that sacrificing the future for the present isn't wise. Social norms remind us that procrastination is not beneficial for us or others. So why do we do it? Why do we procrastinate despite knowing that it is irrational and goes against societal values?

Answering these pressing questions is the focus of this chapter and Chapter 6. We examine the latest evidence and scientific insights into when and why people procrastinate through the lens of short-term mood repair to delve into the deeper reasons why people procrastinate despite knowing it will cause harm. We'll look below the surface at the psychological processes underlying our urges to procrastinate and examine how apparent laziness, lack of motivation, or poor time management skills are a cover-up for our struggle to manage our emotions. We also examine how and why our emotional states are tethered to our perceptions of time and how this can keep us trapped in a pattern of making temporally shortsighted trade-offs when it comes to our goals.

With these insights in hand, we then unpack the sources of the negative emotions that can drive procrastination and highlight how to become more aware of these sources so we can learn to deal with them more effectively. Last, we touch on the perennial nature-versus-nurture question as it relates to procrastination from a mood regulation perspective. Together, these evidence-based insights will provide you with the knowledge you need to understand your own procrastination. Once you are equipped with this understanding, you will find it easier to take a more compassionate view of procrastination so that you can then begin to take steps toward tackling it and leading a more satisfying, productive life.

WHAT'S MOOD GOT TO DO WITH IT?

As someone who researches procrastination, I frequently receive interview requests from journalists and bloggers to answer questions about procrastination and why people do it. They inevitably ask me about how time management and willpower play a role in procrastination. They ask for tips on how people can reduce distractions and organize their working time better to combat procrastination. It's usually at this point that I stop them and get to enjoy a bit of myth-busting. I tell them that, contrary to what many people think, pro-crastination isn't due to laziness, or a lack of focus, or poor impulse control. It's about poor mood management, not poor time manage-ment. If you consider that our emotions are anything but rational, then this makes perfect sense. Procrastination is irrational. And it's irrational because our emotions—and, more specifically, our diffi-culties in managing emotions—are central to understanding when and why people procrastinate.

The idea that emotions, and not poor planning, or laziness, or poor time management skills, are key to understanding and addressing procrastination can be a bit of a shocker at first for most people. After all, the popular press, self-help gurus, and productivity coaches have been promoting for years the idea that getting more organized, removing distractions, and other similar rational approaches are what's needed to get your procrastination under control. Create better to-do lists, unplug from social media, shore up your will-power, and learn to delay your gratification, and soon you will have a procrastination-free life! Well, maybe not quite. Although it's true that these quick fixes can in some cases appear to provide imme-diate relief from procrastination, for most people this relief is likely to be short lived. Why? Because these approaches only scratch the surface of the problem. They focus on the symptoms of procrastina-tion rather than the root causes.

To illustrate, imagine there is a difficult conversation you need to have with a friend about a planned getaway coming up next month. Your friend is counting on you to join them on this trip to a destination that you have agreed on, but now you aren't really that thrilled about it. But every time you pick up your smartphone to call and let them know about your change of heart, you end up instead responding to notifications from your social media or following the clickbait from your news feed. This goes on for days, until the deadline for changing the travel arrangements without losing money is upon you. In short, you've procrastinated.

What happened here? Well, we might want to say that you were a victim of the digital distractions, and this was the cause of your procrastination. It's easy and convenient to blame outside circumstances. As we discuss in Chapter 10, the environment can make it easier to procrastinate. On its own, though, the environment doesn't cause anyone to procrastinate.

If we want to understand the deeper reasons for our procrastination, we need to peel back the layers to reveal the truth behind this irrational behavior. We need to keep asking "Why?" So, *why* were you distracted? You might then answer that you found the digital distractions more interesting than calling your friend. Relative to calling your friend to back out of the trip, watching cute kitten YouTube videos was more enjoyable. But *why*, then, were you choosing to do something more enjoyable than calling your friend? You might reflect on this and conclude that calling your friend to discuss the vacation was not something you enjoyed doing. But why didn't you enjoy doing it? You might then realize that thinking about calling your friend made you feel anxious and worried about whether your excuse to back out would be good enough and whether your friend would understand your reasoning and continue the friendship regardless. Surfing online shops and watching funny videos took you away from those unpleasant feelings, at least for a little while. An emotions researcher might say it gave you a *positive hedonic shift*. It helped you manage those feelings, temporarily, but at the cost of being honest with your friend and doing so in time to recoup the vacation expenses.

We could apply this same approach of asking "Why?" to any number of other apparent causes of procrastination. Whether you're avoiding a task because you've been busy doing other, less important or pressing tasks, or whether it's because you think that you will be more productive if you work on the task at some other future time, or even at the last minute, if you keep asking "Why?" you will eventually arrive at the same reason. You're not doing the task because it is connected to unpleasant, negative emotional states. Now, we could go even further, and peel back yet another layer and ask why the task gives rise to such unpleasant, negative emotions, but that's a discussion for Chapter 6.

Are You Avoiding the Task or Those Unpleasant Emotions?

The preceding example illustrates that when we dig deeper, the truth about why we procrastinate becomes clearer. We are not simply avoiding a task; we are in fact avoiding the negative emotions linked to the task. In essence, when you procrastinate you are managing your emotions by avoiding a task that triggers unpleasant, negative emotions.

Research on the types of tasks people procrastinate tells the same story. Evidence has consistently shown that people procrastinate when they find a task to be aversive or unpleasant (e.g., Blunt & Pychyl, 2000). Whether it's a small or large task, if you find it to be stressful, anxiety provoking, difficult, frustrating, unpleasant, lacking in meaning, or just plain boring you are more likely to procrastinate that task than one that you don't find to be aversive. Encountering an unpleasant or threatening task is necessary, but not sufficient, for procrastination to take place. Something else has to be going on, or humankind would have been stopped dead in our tracks (quite literally) thousands of years ago when we encountered food shortages, difficulties with predators, competing tribes, or other unpleasant challenges.

This makes sense if we consider the flip side of the coin. How often have you have had the urge to procrastinate a task that you really enjoyed, felt enthusiastic about, or that was simply fun? Rarely or never? Exactly. We don't usually procrastinate tasks that we enjoy or that are pleasant, only those we find unpleasant or aversive. If doing home repairs and making renovations is something you really enjoy doing, then it's unlikely you will procrastinate those tasks. But for the rest of us, who may find that even thinking about renovating the kitchen induces a state of boredom, stress, dread, or anxiety, it's more likely that we will procrastinate on repairing that kitchen cabinet. When we put aside a home repair that is making us anxious, we are also putting aside all those stressful and anxious feelings, at least for the moment. When we do so, we get an immediate reward in the form of relief from those unpleasant emotions. And if we decide to do something more enjoyable instead, we get the added bonus of shifting our negative mood to a positive one. By making this hedonic shift, we are engaging in a form of emotion regulation.

Recall that in Chapter 1 we discussed the idea that procrastination, by definition, reflects a *self-regulation* failure. Self-regulation involves the steps you take to manage and marshal your thoughts, emotions, and behaviors so that you can do what is necessary to achieve your goals. The things you do to regulate your emotions fall under the umbrella of self-regulation and inevitably play a key role in how successful you are in regulating your behaviors. For emotion regulation to be successful, it needs to be effective. In other words, the things you do to manage your emotions need to help, not hinder, your efforts to reach your goals. The strategies you use to regulate your emotions—for example, to dial down negative feelings and dial up positive feelings—also need to have lasting, not temporary, effects. Quick fixes don't count when it comes to truly effective emotion regulation.

From this perspective, procrastination simply does not make the cut as an effective emotion regulation strategy. When you avoid making those home repairs or renovations to manage the negative feelings you have about them, you impede your progress toward your goal. Moreover, disengaging from fixing that kitchen cabinet by doing something distracting or more pleasant will give you only temporary relief from your feelings of frustration, boredom, or stress.

It is true that the alternative tasks you choose to do while procrastinating may help dial up your positive feelings. Who doesn't feel better after watching cute kitten videos? But when you next attempt to pull out the tools to fix that cabinet, it's more than likely that all those same unpleasant feelings of frustration, anxiety, self-doubt, and so on that drove you to procrastinate in the first place will still be there, waiting for you like a bad but catchy song that you can't get seem to get out of your head. What it ultimately comes down to is that, emotionally, procrastination is not a sustainable habit.

It's also important to remember that the negative emotions we associate with a task can fall along a continuum in intensity, ranging from boredom; to mild frustration; to full-on, gut-wrenching anxiety and stress. Everyone's threshold for tolerating and managing negative emotions differs. What triggers an urge to procrastinate for you will not be the same as it is for someone else. For example, procrastination can depend on whether you are confident that you can effectively manage these emotions because you have done so in the past. If you don't believe that you have the capacity to manage a certain negative emotion well, then you will be less likely to attempt to tackle it head on. Instead, you will be more likely to resort to using a strategy that helps you avoid the experience of that emotion. In other words, you will procrastinate.

Take a Moment

Let's pause briefly to reflect on tasks you might be procrastinating. Ask yourself: "How do I feel when I think about this task?" "Are my emotions negative?" "How intense are they?" "How confident am I that I can manage these emotions without resorting to procrastination?" To help you visualize how you feel about this task, use the "Emotion Meter" in Figure 5.1 and imagine where you would place the needle for each of the tasks that you may be tempted to procrastinate.

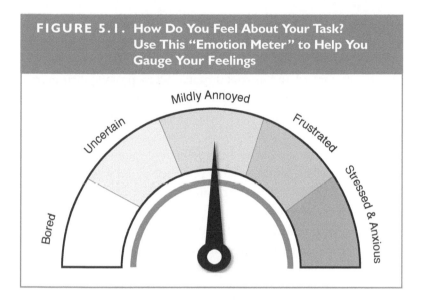

FIGURE 5.1. How Do You Feel About Your Task? Use This "Emotion Meter" to Help You Gauge Your Feelings

What If You Couldn't Change Your Mood?

A very clever research study conducted by Diane Tice and her colleagues (Tice et al., 2001) provides one of the best demonstrations of how our beliefs about our ability to manage and self-regulate our emotions can influence whether we procrastinate. In that study, the researchers first gave participants a mood induction task that involved reading either a story with a sad ending or one with a happy ending, to make the participants feel sad or happy.

The participants were next told that they had to wait 15 minutes before finishing the experiment but, in the meantime, the researchers asked them if they wouldn't mind helping out with a pilot study that involved taste testing pretzels, chocolate chip cookies, and Goldfish crackers. They could eat as much as they needed to be able to evaluate the taste of the snacks. However, there was a catch: Some of the participants were told that whatever mood they were in now, this was the mood in which they were likely to stay for the rest of the experiment. They were told that eating would not do anything to change their mood and instead it would likely prolong their current mood. This was an important point to make because many people use food to try to change their mood. Just think about the last time you indulged in a pint of Ben & Jerry's ice cream when you were feeling down or when you ate one too many cookies after a hard day. In effect, the participants were told that their mood was "frozen" and could not be changed, even by eating.

What the researchers found was fascinating: The participants who were made to feel sad and who were not given any instructions about their mood being frozen ate more than those who were told that eating wouldn't change their mood. In essence, if participants believed that there wasn't anything they could do to change their sad mood, they were better at exercising their self-control and didn't overindulge in the snacks. They accepted their mood and just carried on with the experiment. In contrast, sad participants who expected that eating might help repair their mood were more susceptible to the temptation of eating, and so they ate more.

These intriguing results provide some important insights into why and how emotions can get in the way of our efforts to self-regulate. When we are experiencing negative emotions, we will actively do things to try and regulate our emotions. If we are exposed to something tempting that we believe might help us dial down those negative emotions, then we are more likely to use it to repair our mood, even if it means doing something that may work against our long-term goals. If we haven't developed the internal resources or skills to help us manage those negative emotions on our own, and effectively regulate them, then we use external sources to help dial them down. We distract ourselves with enjoyable pastimes, social media, playing video games, and so on so that we don't have to keep experiencing the stress, frustration, anxiety, boredom, or dread that we feel when we engage with *that* task.

It's important to mention, though, that negative emotions on their own are not always a bad thing and can actually be useful. From the perspective of self-regulation, negative emotions provide us valuable feedback about how we are getting on with respect to our goals. For example, if you are feeling frustrated while working on a task, those feelings of frustration tell you that you have encountered an obstacle in your path toward your goal. This can signal to you that you may require more information, a different approach, or more resources to successfully complete the task. However, if you respond to those negative feelings by avoiding them and procrastinating, rather than with curiosity and acceptance, then you miss opportunities to harness those feelings to make progress. In Chapter 7, we delve more into why accepting your negative feelings is important for fostering self-compassion and reducing procrastination, and in Chapter 8, we address how to approach and decode your negative emotions about a task into something meaningful and manageable.

WHAT'S TIME (ORIENTATION) GOT TO DO WITH IT?

From our discussion so far, it should make sense why I have suggested that procrastination is a form of self-regulation failure that involves prioritizing short-term mood repair over the long-term pursuit of intended actions. When we procrastinate, we focus more on finding ways to repair a negative mood linked to a task than on making progress toward our goals. Regardless of whether these goals will come to fruition in the near, middle, or far future, we miss out on opportunities to reach them when we spend our precious time managing our mood rather than taking action to get our tasks done. That time can't be recovered. Unless you happen to be lucky enough to have a time machine, you can't get back time spent on getting temporary relief from unpleasant tasks by procrastinating. This is why time can be considered the only truly nonrenewable resource we have. Once we spend it, it's gone—for good.

A view of procrastination from this perspective further highlights its irrationality. When we procrastinate, we make a temporal trade-off. Whether we are fully aware of it or not, we are sacrificing the future for the present. We are squandering our time, a resource that we can't replenish, for the sake of our emotions. This is not to say that emotions are not important—far from it. Of course, it's important that we find healthy ways to manage our emotions. Countless research studies have shown that we tend to make better decisions, are more creative, and more productive when our negative emotions aren't running amok. As we noted earlier, though, healthy emotion regulation needs to be both effective and have lasting effects. As an emotion regulation strategy, procrastination provides neither.

Moreover, after we have procrastinated we are often all too aware of the fact that we have lost valuable time and that the deadline to get a particular task done is swiftly approaching (or perhaps it has already made that swooshing sound as it passed us by). Not surprisingly, this can lead to feeling time pressured or time starved, and when we feel we don't have enough time to do something, we feel stressed. Recall from Chapter 3 that procrastination is linked to higher levels of stress. When you feel stressed about a task you are more likely to procrastinate it. But when you procrastinate, you are also more likely to feel stressed. This is in part because you realize that you have lost precious time that could have been better spent on getting your task done and meeting your deadlines. Consider the following quote from a research participant:

> Some deadlines are so far into the future [that] the consequence of this is you feel you have time to address it at a later time. However, as the deadline approaches panic sets in and I can focus on nothing else and reprimand myself for allowing so much time to pass and putting myself in an unnecessary stressful situation.

This quote highlights two crucial points that underscore the temporal self-regulation failure involved in procrastination. First, our perceptions of how close or far away the future feels have a direct relevance for procrastination. In this example, the person explains that they put their task off because the deadline seemed to be so far in the future. This gave them the illusion that there was plenty of time left to work on it some other time. Second, ignoring the fact that this person is blaming their procrastination on their perception of time rather than on any negative emotions that were driving them to put off the task in the first place, their observation happens to be supported by scientific evidence, which we discuss next.

The Present Is Real, the Future Is Imagined

Research on how we perceive time indicates that we tend to think about the present in more concrete terms than we do the future. This makes sense if we consider that the present is tangible to us—we have direct experiences of the present moment through each of our five senses. This makes the present concrete and real. The future, on the other hand, is filled with seemingly endless possibilities and outcomes. We can only imagine what our circumstances will be, and what we will be like, in the future. Even if we were to choose one of the myriad ways we could imagine that the future could play out for us, for most of us the future feels much more abstract and less concrete than the present. And the more abstract and farther away in time something seems to us, the more psychologically distant it feels to us as well. So, when a deadline is not in our immediate future, it can feel farther away than it actually is.

The connection between how abstract versus concrete our perceptions of events and activities are, and whether we view them as near or far away on the temporal horizon, is not one way. In fact, research has shown that when we describe an activity in more abstract than concrete terms we are more likely to view it as being distant from us, both temporally and psychologically. We, in turn, are more likely to procrastinate it. These points were demonstrated in a series of studies in which researchers asked participants to respond to an email questionnaire within 3 weeks (McCrea et al., 2008). Some participants were given questionnaires that were designed to induce a more concrete way of thinking, whereas others were given questionnaires to induce thinking about their task in more abstract ways. Which group of participants do you think returned their questionnaire earlier and didn't delay the task? Well, if you deduced that it was the group who received the questionnaire with concrete-thinking instructions, give yourself a pat on the back. Those who were given instructions that induced a more abstract way of thinking returned their questionnaires much later.

However, if you also started thinking that this study perhaps actually didn't test procrastination, congratulations—you are right! What the researchers tested was most likely delay, not procrastination. We have no evidence that the participants intended to perform this task, or that completing and returning the questionnaire was important to them, or that their delay was voluntary and unnecessary. Despite these issues, procrastination is indeed a form of delay. So, in principle, thinking about a task in more concrete terms may help reduce procrastination as well as delay. But again, this evidence doesn't fully answer the question of why we want to put that task off in the first place.

What this research does highlight, though, is how viewing different time frames as being more or less tangible may factor into procrastination. If you think of the future as being abstract and intangible, then it will feel farther away. Viewing the future this way can give the illusion that you have more time to complete a task, in much the same way that was described in the quote I presented earlier in this chapter. This, in turn, can make it easier for you to justify unnecessarily delaying that task when you are wrangling with the frustration, stress, resentment, boredom, or anxiety you are experiencing as you struggle with the task.

When we procrastinate, we view the future as being more abstract than concrete. But this also means that your Future Self, the temporal versions of your self that will exist at a given future time, also won't feel as real. Instead, your Future Self will feel more like a stranger than a close friend. This is due in part to the tendency that people have to equate temporal distance with psychological distance.

Take a Moment

To illustrate these ideas, let's try a thought experiment. Take a moment to imagine your Future Self of tomorrow. Imagine this Future Self and how similar or different that Future You of tomorrow is compared with Present You. Next, try to imagine your Future Self 1 month from now. How similar or different is this Future You of 1 month from now compared with who you are today? If you had to rate how emotionally and psychologically close you feel to each of these Future Selves, what score would you give each? The series of overlapping circles in Figure 5.2 can help you visualize this. A score of 1 would mean that your Future Self feels very distant psychologically, like a stranger (top left circles). A score of 7 would mean that your Future Self feels very familiar, like a close friend (bottom right circles).

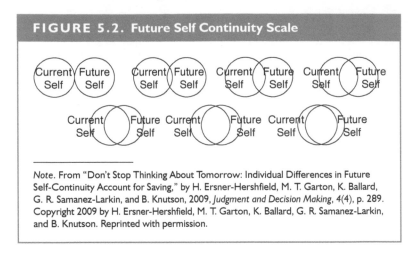

FIGURE 5.2. Future Self Continuity Scale

Note. From "Don't Stop Thinking About Tomorrow: Individual Differences in Future Self-Continuity Account for Saving," by H. Ersner-Hershfield, M. T. Garton, K. Ballard, G. R. Samanez-Larkin, and B. Knutson, 2009, *Judgment and Decision Making*, 4(4), p. 289. Copyright 2009 by H. Ersner-Hershfield, M. T. Garton, K. Ballard, G. R. Samanez-Larkin, and B. Knutson. Reprinted with permission.

How Close Do You Feel to Your Future Self?

If you are like most people, you probably gave your 1-day Future Self a higher score than you did your 1-month Future Self in the thought experiment. This is, to some extent, to be expected. After all, 1-month Future You *is* less concrete and real than Present You. Now, if you were to continue this thought experiment and consider how close you would feel to 1-year Future You, your score likely would be even lower than the one you gave for 1-month Future You. The further away in time that Future You is, the less close and more psychologically distant from you it seems. This thought experiment demonstrates that the more distant in time our Future Self is, the less connected we feel to that Future Self. In other words, that distant Future Self is more like a stranger than a close friend. Moreover, research suggests that, for many of us, this is the default way of thinking.

Consider, for example, research that has examined the neural correlates of how we think about our Future Self. Using functional magnetic resonance imaging, or fMRI, as it's commonly referred to, researchers have found that a particular area of the brain, the medial prefrontal cortex, shows heightened activation when we think about self-relevant information (Hershfield, 2011). Using fMRI, researchers also found that when people think about their own qualities and traits and those that apply to other people, this area of the brain shows more activity when people think of their own traits and less activity when they think of other people's traits (Kelley et al., 2002).

What do you think happens when people think about the traits and qualities that apply to a distant Future Self? Well, researchers found that the neural activation pattern was, in general, strangely similar to the pattern observed when they think about other people's traits (Ersner-Hershfield et al., 2009). In other words, when people thought about and described a distant Future Self their neural activity was the same as when they were describing Brad Pitt or Jennifer Lopez. Their Future Self was essentially a stranger.

Although this can be the default pattern for many people, researchers have discovered that a quite different pattern is observed in other people. In the same research I just described, some participants who were asked to think about the traits and qualities of their Future Self displayed a pattern of brain activation that was more consistent with the pattern of neural activation seen when they think about themselves. For these individuals, the Future Self is seen as being more similar than dissimilar to their Present Self. Researchers such as Hal Hershfield at the University of California, Los Angeles, refer to this as *future self-continuity*. Future Self is viewed as being more like a close friend than a stranger.

This isn't the case, however, when we procrastinate. Research that I have conducted has consistently found that people who are prone to procrastinating report feeling more emotionally and psychologically distant from their Future Self than those who are less apt to procrastinate. In one study, my colleagues and I found that feeling less connected to one's Future Self explained in part why people who were prone to procrastinate were also less likely to regularly engage in a range of health-promoting behaviors, such as healthy eating, regular exercise, avoiding junk food, and getting a good night's sleep (Sirois et al., 2014). When you view your Future Self as a stranger, someone who is distant psychologically and emotionally from you, it becomes easier to disregard how your current actions (or lack thereof) can affect your Future Self. You can be less concerned about the well-being of this not-yet-real future version of yourself.

Superhero or Beast of Burden?

Being out of sync with our Future Self can also make it easier to make the temporal trade-offs that lead to procrastination. After all, it's easy to disregard the consequences of our unnecessary delay if we view them as happening to a future version of ourselves that feels so psychologically and emotionally distant from us that it may as well be happening to someone else, so why not put off that difficult task to a future time? Future You can deal with it and any fallout from the delay, right?

But there's another reason why we might be so quick to push forward our difficult and unpleasant tasks to our Future Self. If our Future Self seems abstract and psychologically distant to us, then we also tend to view that Future Self as being *temporally* distant from us. In other words, we perceive that this version of ourselves is farther away in time from the present moment. And because we tend to equate the passage of time with self-improvement, it's easier to imagine that this Future Self will be a much better person than you are now. Numerous studies have demonstrated this fascinating effect (e.g., Ross & Wilson, 2003). Distant Past Selves are seen as having more negative characteristics compared with the Present Self, and Distant Future Selves are judged to have more positive qualities than the Present Self.

To illustrate, let's say that you have to write an important report that is due in 2 weeks. Present You is struggling with writing the report and feeling very stressed as a result. So, what do you do? Well, if you don't feel particularly close to your Future Self, it's easy to justify putting aside working on that report. After all, Future You will have more energy, better ideas, more willpower, and more motivation and be better able to manage all those negative emotions that you can't right now. We have a natural bias toward seeing ourselves as improving over time—Future You will be much better at all the things that current you is struggling with, right? So, this makes it okay to put your unfinished task in the capable hands of Superhero Future You.

Let's fast forward to 1 week from now. Future You is Present You and now has to struggle with writing the report that the now–Past You procrastinated. Unfortunately, that 1-week–Future You doesn't have more energy, better ideas, willpower, or motivation than what Past You, who procrastinated, did. Future You is still just you and is struggling with all the same negative emotions that Past You tried to escape by procrastinating. Future You hasn't miraculously transformed into some superhero version of yourself to swoop in and save the day. Yet because you felt very disconnected from this Future You, you believed that Future You would be very different. In effect, you overestimated how much you would change over a short period of time. And now your Future Self has to pay the price.

When you consign the work of today to your Future Self, you make that Future Self your beast of burden. Your Future Self has to bear the weight of the consequences of all your lost time and unnecessary delays. Put differently, when you place the responsibility of dealing with your difficult tasks on the shoulders of your Future Self, you are stealing time from them (with "them" being a future version of yourself). In other words, you aren't treating your Future Self with kindness, compassion, or consideration. You're expecting a lot of them, more than you do from your Present Self.

Instead of using our time now to work on the important task we need to get done, we squander it on doing something else. This means we leave less time for our Future Self to actually get the task done. We time-starve our Future Self. And when we feel time-starved, we feel stressed.

Why It's Difficult to Consider How Your Future Self Will Feel When You Procrastinate

You may be wondering at this point what our perception of time has to do with our emotions. We know that procrastination is a form of temporal self-regulation failure that means we put greater importance on the needs of our Present Self than those of our Future Self. The scientific evidence also tells us that if we're prone to procrastination, thinking about the future and our Future Self who will be existing in that future is not something that comes easily.

This raises an important question about procrastination: Why is it that even when we realize that our procrastination has put our goals in jeopardy, and that we are causing hardship to our Future Self, we still get trapped into prioritizing the present over the future? Why do we continue to resolve such temporal dilemmas at the expense of our Future Self?

One intriguing explanation to this puzzle involves the way our thinking changes when we feel threatened, anxious, or stressed. When we encounter something in the environment that threatens our well-being, the amygdala is activated. This small, almond-shaped structure in our brain serves as a threat detector that sets off the stress reaction, also known as the *fight-or-flight response*. This response involves a cascade of physiological, biochemical, and behavioral changes that evolved to help us deal automatically with life-threatening events and survive the harsh, primitive world of early humankind. As the term "fight or flight" implies, this response provides the impetus to either face head on any potential threat or remove ourselves from danger by fleeing and avoiding the threat. Although the modern-day "threats" that we experience rarely involve events that jeopardize our survival, this same stress response is set in motion whether the threat is a pending report deadline or an approaching predator. Either one will activate the amygdala.

Although the amygdala is involved in the regulation of emotions more generally, a key function that has particular relevance to understanding how we think about time is its role in vigilance. The amygdala helps orient our attention to threats in the environment so that we can be prepared to deal with them. This translates into increased vigilance for and rapid detection of the negative aspects of our environment. For example, when we encounter a stressor, the amygdala orients our attention quickly toward it so that we can take appropriate action (fight or flight).

That's not all the amygdala does, though. Once we have detected a threat, we also want to keep a close eye on that threat so that it doesn't cause further harm. This makes sense from an evolutionary perspective, but this is also why our activated amygdala will make it harder to disengage from that threat. It orients our focus to any negative stimuli in the here-and-now until the pending threat to our well-being is successfully dealt with. When our focus is mainly on the present moment, and narrowly directed toward detecting any further threats to our well-being, it can be difficult to think about the future, let alone our Future Self.

This threat-induced shortsightedness can be thought of as a *temporal myopia*. In much the same way that medical myopia (or *nearsightedness*, as it's often referred to) can make it difficult to see objects in the distance clearly, temporal myopia can make it difficult to consider what the future consequences of our current actions will be. Our temporal shortsightedness means that we don't factor the future or our Future Self into our decision making. Our focus is primarily on the present and how to manage the threats we feel we are facing. But we think less about how our Future Self will feel when they have to deal with the aftermath of our current procrastination. In Chapter 9 we look at some strategies that you can use to make it easier to think about your Future Self and how they feel when we procrastinate.

CORRECTIVE LENSES TO PUT YOUR FUTURE SELF BACK INTO FOCUS

Temporal myopia—shortsightedness—can easily develop into a vicious cycle. If you're feeling stressed, anxious, or threatened about a task you have to do, your focus will be on trying to reduce these feelings now. The temporal myopia induced by these feelings will also make it harder to think about the consequences to your Future Self of procrastinating. Disengaging from the task now to gain some relief from these uncomfortable feelings then becomes the best option. After you have procrastinated, you feel stressed because you've wasted time and time-starved your Future Self. Then the whole cycle starts again.

Thankfully, you can take several steps to help break this vicious cycle. One involves asking yourself questions, such as those in the "What Are Your Thoughts and Feelings Toward Your Future Self?" exercise. Use these questions as a starting point to help you become more aware of why you see your Future Self as an abstract, intangible superhero version of yourself. Think of these questions as a metaphoric set of corrective lenses that help bring your Future Self closer into focus. When you realize that your Future Self is not that much different from your Present Self, it will be harder to fall into the trap of pushing off to Future You the responsibility for today's challenging tasks.

EXERCISE: What Are Your Thoughts and Feelings Toward Your Future Self?

It might seem odd to take stock of a Future version of yourself before that Future You even exists, but this is exactly the approach that is needed to uncover some of the thoughts and feelings you have about that Future Self that may be perpetuating a cycle of procrastination.

Think about a task you have been procrastinating or that you are tempted to procrastinate. Take a few quiet moments to reflect on each of the following questions in relation to that task before answering.

1. Why will Future You be better at handling this task than Present You? Fill in the blanks below to help describe why you think Future You may be better equipped to handle the task Present You is struggling with now.
   a) Future Me will be more _____ than Present Me.
   b) Future Me will be better at _____ than Present Me.
   c) Future Me will have more _____ than Present Me.
   d) Future Me will feel more _____ than Present Me.
   e) Future Me will feel less _____ than Present Me.

2. When in the future does the Future You that you described above exist?
   _____ days _____ weeks _____ months _____ years

3. How much do you expect that you will change as a person during this time frame?
   ___ a great deal ___ somewhat ___ a little ___ not much at all

4. Now review each of your above answers to Question 1. As you review your answers, consider the following questions:
   a) How realistic or accurate are these beliefs about your Future Self given the time between now and when that Future You will exist?
   b) Will the Future You that you are putting the task off to really be that much different than who you are right now?
   c) Will the unpleasant feelings that you face now with this task disappear by the time Future You has to deal with the task?

Completing the exercise will help remind you that Future You is just a different temporal version of Present You. Bringing this awareness to the forefront when you are struggling with a task can make it easier to find ways of managing your emotions that don't involve pushing them on to your Future Self. In Chapter 9 we take an in-depth look at several other evidence-based techniques so that you can continue to develop a better relationship with your Future Self and reduce your procrastination.

By this point, I hope you see that this short-term mood regulation view of procrastination puts procrastination in a different light. It reminds us that procrastination is not being driven by wanting to have fun, or being lazy, or shirking responsibility. It's actually being driven by suffering and distress, which are not resolved but passed onto our Future Self. This is all the more reason why you need to be gentle rather than harsh with yourself when you are struggling with procrastination.

CHAPTER 6

SEEK THE SOURCE

Our doubts are traitors, And make us lose the good we oft might win, by fearing to attempt.
—William Shakespeare

In this chapter, you will learn

- why blaming procrastination on the task doesn't fully answer why you procrastinate;
- why even the smallest of tasks can become a source of negative feelings and procrastination;
- to recognize when low self-esteem, perfectionism, and self-criticism can send you on the path to procrastination; and
- how to understand and tackle the source of the negative emotions that promote procrastination.

In the last chapter, we explored procrastination as involving difficulties with emotion regulation. We delved into the dynamics of short-term mood regulation and the costs of this strategy for your Future Self. But if we really want to get a fuller understanding of procrastination and how best to deal with it we need to go further and ask a very important question: "If procrastination is about difficulty managing negative moods and emotions, then where do these negative states come from?"

When you can answer this question, you'll better understand the source of your own and others' procrastination. You'll gain insights that will put you in a much better position to decide which strategies will be most effective for managing the negative emotions that fuel procrastination. Answering this question is the focus of this chapter.

In this chapter, we use psychological science to better understand where the negative emotions that drive us to procrastinate come from. In seeking the source of these negative emotions, we consider two main contributors: (a) how we evaluate the task itself and (b) how we evaluate ourselves in relation to the task.

BLAME IT ON THE TASK?

I noted previously that encountering an unpleasant or aversive task is a necessary but not sufficient condition for procrastination. People don't often procrastinate starting tasks that are considered enjoyable or fun. Why? Because when we are faced with a task that we view as pleasurable or enjoyable we usually have no need to manage our negative emotions. Either we simply aren't experiencing any negative emotions, or the levels are very low relative to the positive feelings we have about the task. In either case, mood regulation isn't needed.

This isn't the case when we are faced with a task that we initially see as being unpleasant, though. Tasks that we view as being boring, frustrating, stressful, difficult, or some other flavor of aversiveness are more likely to be procrastinated. By procrastinating, we get to temporarily put aside the unpleasant emotions we experience when we try to engage with this task. And although reorganizing your filing system may be something that is incredibly boring and unpleasant for some people (myself included!), it may actually be quite enjoyable for others.

Although it's true that there are some clear differences between people in terms of what constitutes an aversive task, the reason why we might view a particular task as unpleasant or aversive isn't completely subjective. Researchers have found that tasks that have certain qualities tend to be commonly viewed as being aversive and in turn are more likely to be procrastinated.

Consider, for example, one study in which researchers asked participants about how they felt about their personal projects (Blunt & Pychyl, 1998). These could be big projects, such as renovating the kitchen, or small projects, such as mailing a refund claim. They then instructed the participants to rate their thoughts and feelings about each of these projects along a number of positive and negative dimensions. The participants' ratings of their projects were then organized according to whether the participants were action oriented or more prone to procrastination. Not surprisingly, those who were more prone to procrastination rated their projects differently across most of the dimensions. These individuals experienced more boredom, guilt, and frustration toward their projects than did those who were action oriented. Such negative emotional states can set the stage for procrastination.

Participants who were prone to procrastination also viewed their projects in other ways that were quite distinctive from those who were less likely to unnecessarily delay a task. Compared with participants who were more action oriented, they saw their projects as being more uncertain, less controllable, and less likely to be completed. This makes sense if we consider that most people feel stressed when they are in circumstances that are uncertain and uncontrollable. So, if you feel unsure about what to do next to progress with your task, or you feel that you have little control over the task (or both), then you likely will feel some degree of stress that can prompt you to procrastinate. Add a dash of low confidence that you will actually be able to finish the task, and you have a recipe for procrastination.

But these weren't the only project dimensions that differed between participants who were prone to procrastination and those who were action oriented. Participants who were prone to procrastinate saw their projects as being less reflective of their sense of identity and found their projects to be less absorbing; in other words, they did not view their projects as tasks that truly reflected their core values. As a result, they found it harder to get deeply involved or engrossed in the project in a meaningful manner. When we have trouble connecting with a task on a deeper personal level, we are also more likely to view that task as boring. After all, boredom is an unpleasant state that reflects a lack of interest.

Think about the last time that you found yourself deeply involved in a task. It may have been while you were gardening, or going for a run, or even writing. It's most likely that you were able to get so absorbed in what you were doing simply because that task held personal meaning for you on some level. Perhaps it resonated with your love of nature, your desire to stay fit and healthy, or your enjoyment of seeing your abstract ideas take shape in concrete form.

Regardless of the specific reason, research has shown that when people connect with a task in a meaningful way they are more likely to allow themselves to become absorbed in the flow of the task. Of course, you have to first view a task as offering you the opportunity to become deeply absorbed in it. But when this does happen, you'll be eager to throw yourself into that task rather than avoid it by procrastinating. In Chapter 9, we revisit this idea of task meaning and how to connect with a task to reduce the chances of procrastination.

PROCRASTINATION AND THE TASK JOURNEY

There's another important quality of tasks that we need to consider if we want to understand why a task may prompt an urge to procrastinate. If we go back to our basic definition of procrastination, you'll notice that it hints at when procrastination occurs: "Procrastination is a common self-regulation problem involving the unnecessary and voluntary delay in the start or completion of important intended tasks despite the recognition that this delay may have negative consequences." Procrastination involves delay in *starting or completing* an intended task. This means there are multiple opportunities to procrastinate not only before we start the task but also while we are working on a task.

All tasks and goals have different stages, with some being easier and more enjoyable than others. It is easy to see how this would be true for bigger tasks or those that have a number of moving parts. We might be very enthused to start that kitchen renovation because we can envision how much better it will look than our current, outdated kitchen once it's refurbished. But once we get started and see that the work involved is much more complex and costly than we had anticipated, feelings of frustration, uncertainty, and stress can creep in and replace that initial enthusiasm. It's at this stage of the project that we will be more likely to procrastinate.

For example, in one survey of more than 2,000 homeowners in the United States, 32% had put off one or more home improvement projects for more than 12 months (Schmall, 2018). Whether it was remodeling the bathroom or kitchen or simply repainting a room, homeowners in this survey admitted to abandoning their projects halfway through because it became too much for them to deal with. Now yes, there may be some very practical reasons for putting of that do-it-yourself project or renovation, such as lack of time or money. In many cases, though, the reason for procrastination is simply that the emotions people had about a particular stage of the task shifted from being pleasant to much more unpleasant.

The reasons why we might see a task as more or less aversive can also wax and wane throughout the life of a project. In one study, researchers asked participants to generate a list of projects on which they were currently working and rate them using the same method I described earlier in this chapter (Blunt & Pychyl, 2000). This time, though, they also asked them to indicate the stage they were at with their project, from being just conceived but not yet started to completed.

As expected, the researchers found that at each stage of the project procrastination was associated with seeing the task as aversive. So, regardless of whether people were about to start, were in the planning stage, were taking action on their project, or were nearing completion, they experienced feelings of boredom, resentment, and frustration. As you would expect, these unpleasant feelings fueled the urge to procrastinate.

But there were also some important differences between the project stages in terms of how the participants rated their projects on other important dimensions. At the inception stage, when they were about to initiate the project, task aversiveness was associated with seeing the project as having less personal meaning. In other words, projects at this stage were more likely to be aversive if they were seen as not being fun, enjoyable, or linked to one's identity. Feelings of stress and other negative emotions were also prominent at this stage and fed into seeing the project as aversive.

The researchers also found evidence that the reasons why we might see a task as more or less aversive shifts when we start to take action. For tasks that people were actively engaged in, feeling that there was little control over the task and feeling uncertain about some aspect of the task fed into their perceptions of the task as aversive. Recall that lack of control and certainty are two key ingredients for feeling stressed. Now imagine that you've mustered up enough motivation to push through your initial uncomfortableness about starting a task only to find that you have to execute the task in way that is completely different from how you would normally do it. In other words, you have very little sense of autonomy over the task, and, to make matters worse, you haven't been given clear instructions on *how* to do it this new way. In such circumstances, stress and frustration are sure to follow.

Tasks over which we feel we have little control and have some degree of uncertainty about can also be seen as lacking structure. With loosely organized or even disorganized tasks, we're not sure what is required to get the task to the next stage. This lack of clarity about what needs to be done next can create a breeding ground for procrastination. In short, task uncertainty is a precursor to procrastination.

This research tells us that the reasons when and why we might view a task as being aversive are not straightforward. We need to consider what stage we are at with the task to get a better understanding of why we might shift from initially seeing a task as not too daunting to viewing it as something that elicits feelings of dread and uncertainty. When we are not sure what to do, or we don't have a strong sense of control over the task, action paralysis takes hold. We need to consider that the sources of our negative emotions about a task can be a bit of a moving target. Our perceptions of the aversiveness or enjoyableness of the task can wax and wane over the life of a project. Once we accept this, we can start to get a clearer understanding of when and why we might be tempted to procrastinate.

MINDSETS AND SELF-DOUBT AND SCRIPTS, OH MY!

When we experience unpleasant emotions, it's easy to blame them on the task. Apart from a select group of people, who really enjoys completing tax returns, writing quarterly reports, or cleaning out the garage? But blaming the task takes the focus off an important source of those negative feelings, namely, how we view ourselves in relation to that task and the meaning that task has for the way we evaluate ourselves. These evaluations can, in turn, take us down difficult roads on our journey toward completing tasks that will most likely end in procrastination.

Consider, for example, "ugh tasks." This term was coined to describe those tasks that stay at the bottom of your to-do lists almost indefinitely. They are tasks that you might view initially as having few short-term rewards, and so it's easy to justify pushing them to the bottom of your list. In most cases, though, this is just smoke and mirrors to cover up the fact that at some level this task triggers unpleasant or threatening feelings in you. Maybe the task brings your insecurities and self-doubts to the surface, or maybe thinking about doing this task reminds you of your own shortcomings, which you'd rather not face, so you put the task off to avoid having to grapple with these feelings. The problem is that, over time, those mildly unpleasant feelings can snowball into much more intense emotions of dread, guilt, and shame when you face up to the fact that you still haven't gotten around to taking care of this task. As these unpleasant feelings grow, so does your urge to continue to procrastinate that task.

The reason why this molehill of an unpleasant task turns into a mountain of negative feelings has little to do with the task in itself. It does, however, have everything to do with how you view yourself in relation to the task. You could view struggling with a task as meaning different things, depending on your mindset. You could see this struggle as a natural part of learning something new or as the chance to get better at something and hone your skills, or you could view it as a signal that you are doing something wrong, that you lack the skills or competence to have everything go smoothly, or as proof that you are a failure. Viewing ourselves in a negative light as we work on a task will lead to the sorts of thoughts and negative scripts about ourselves that amplify any negative feelings we had about the task (and ourselves) in the first place.

We now turn to the three types of negative self-views that can feed into and amplify the negative mood that prompts and intensifies an urge to procrastinate: (a) low self-esteem, (b) perfectionism, and (c) self-criticism. When we engage in negative thinking about ourselves and our tasks in these ways, we feel worse about ourselves and our ability to complete our tasks. This, in turn, can make the journey toward accomplishing our goal that much more difficult and unpleasant. By understanding when and how our negative self-views are operating, we can take steps toward changing our mental scripts and getting back onto a smoother journey toward our goals.

Take a Moment

Let's stop and take a moment. What five qualities or personality characteristics would you use to describe yourself? Try not to think about it too much. Just write down the words that come immediately to mind to fill in the blanks.

"I am someone who is _____, _____, _____, _____, and _____."

You can check the end of this section for further instructions on what to do next.

The Bumpy Road of Low Self-Esteem and the Level Road of Healthy Self-Esteem

If someone asked you whether you had high or low self-esteem, how would you answer? Would you come up with a reply right away, or would it take some thought before you could come up with an answer? The fact is that we rarely think about our self-esteem unless it's brought to our attention. It's something that operates in the background, often in ways that we don't always recognize or understand.

Self-esteem is your sense of self-worth. It reflects the extent to which you value yourself and feel that you are worthy and deserving of rewards and of other people's respect and love. When people have healthy self-esteem, they are better able to deal with life's ups and downs, in part because they don't take things as personally as other people do. Experiencing a failure or lapse doesn't detract from their sense of being a valuable person or taken as meaning that they are a failure. People with high self-esteem have a more stable view of themselves and their worth that isn't easily shaken by minor setbacks. This makes it easier for them to continue with their goals even when everything may not be going smoothly or as planned.

Low self-esteem, though, makes it that much harder to manage your reactions to the inevitable challenges, setbacks, and struggles on the journey toward your goal. Researchers have found some intriguing and very telling differences between people with high and low self-esteem. When everything is going smoothly while they are working toward their goals, people with low self-esteem view their goals in ways that are very similar to those with high self-esteem. Give them an easy puzzle to solve, for example, and all is well. You wouldn't be able to spot the difference between those with high and low self-esteem.

When the journey toward their goal gets a bit rocky, though, people with low self-esteem react much more strongly. If you give people a difficult puzzle to solve, the differences between those with high and low self-esteem becoming glaringly clear (Brown & Dutton, 1995). Those with high self-esteem find the puzzle difficult but tend not to feel too bad about themselves. In contrast, people with low self-esteem interpret their struggle with such challenges as proof that their negative view of themselves is accurate and that they are incompetent or a failure. They tend to feel more shamed, humiliated, and dissatisfied with themselves after even minor difficulties than do people who have a healthier, stronger sense of self-worth. These negative feelings can then feed an urge to procrastinate as a way to cope.

To illustrate, let's imagine you are on a road trip to an important destination. Your trip begins with the usual trek along the highway. You're used to traveling along this highway—the route is familiar, and the road is smooth and easy to travel. Everything is going fine until you hit a detour sign diverting traffic off the highway to unfamiliar side roads through the countryside. Next thing you know, the side roads have turned into a bumpy gravel road. There are potholes, and overall the road is very uneven.

If you have healthy self-esteem, the detour is like driving with a really good set of shocks on your car: Even though the road is bumpy, you know your shocks will absorb most of the bumps and allow you to drive down the road to your destination without being jostled about too much. Self-esteem is like your buffer against the ups and downs of life. This is why people with high self-esteem tend to persist with their goals even after experiencing lapses and setbacks.

If you have low self-esteem, such a detour is like not having any shocks on your car at all. Without any shock absorbers, you feel every pothole and bump along the road, making your journey very difficult and unpleasant. At some point, these jolts and bumps may become so hard to tolerate that you decide to stop your car, turn back, and not reach your destination.

Low self-esteem can contribute to a tendency to procrastinate in much the same way. It can amplify the small difficulties and uncertainties you encounter on the journey toward finishing a task or goal and make them, and you, feel a lot worse. The worse we feel about ourselves in relation to a task, the more likely it is that we will want to avoid that task to escape those difficult and often painful feelings about ourselves.

But there's another dynamic at work here, too. When we procrastinate, we know we are not living up to our commitments. We know we are transgressing the social norms about being a productive member of society. We know we are letting ourselves and others down. These acknowledgments, and any persistent rumination on these realizations, can erode our sense of self-worth. In other words, procrastination may also damage our self-esteem, especially if it wasn't all that high to begin with.

When we have low self-esteem, we have a distorted view of what setbacks and lapses mean. Instead of seeing these difficulties as a natural part of the journey toward our goal, we see them as reflections of our inadequacies, as a reason why we are not worthy of experiencing success or being respected by others. When we have low self-esteem, our internal script maintains negative beliefs about ourselves that are neither realistic nor healthy. We explore some of these negative beliefs and how we can replace them with healthier ones toward the end of this chapter.

The Unrealistic Journey of Perfectionism and the Realistic Road of Striving for Excellence

Most of us live in a society that glorifies high performance and high achievement, that celebrates excellence and rewards people who push beyond the limits of comfort to set new and even higher standards in science, art, and business. "Be better," "Rise higher," and "Reach for the top" are the mantras of our modern world. This striving for excellence is seen as the way to advance knowledge, culture, and society. After all, what progress would we have made as a species if we had just been content with the status quo?

Now, there is nothing wrong with pushing the envelope or striving for excellence. It can be healthy and adaptive to try and reach our full potential and be the best version of ourselves that we can be.

Excelling in academics, or creative pursuits, or sports and exercise, can give us a sense of pride and accomplishment, which in turn can feed a healthy sense of self-esteem.

The problem is that people often mistake perfectionism for these healthy forms of striving for excellence. People who are perfectionists do appear to be trying to improve their performance and striving to be their best. But although it's true that on the surface, perfectionism appears to be about striving for excellence, perfectionism includes other characteristics that can make it anything but healthy.

Perfectionism isn't actually about striving for excellence—that's something researchers refer to as *excellentism*. Instead of striving for just excellence, perfectionists strive for perfection. The problem is that perfection is an idealized concept—it doesn't really exist. Perfection is an illusion. The perfectionist, however, views the perfect performance, the perfect body, or the perfect report as real and attainable. So, if you dedicate to yourself to pursuing a standard that doesn't exist, or is so high it may as well be unreachable, imagine how you will feel about yourself as you find time and again that you have failed to reach your goal.

Before we delve further into how perfectionism can contribute to negative self-views, it's important to point out that perfectionism comes in different forms. The two main forms that are most relevant to our understanding of procrastination are referred to by researchers as (a) *perfectionistic strivings* and (b) *perfectionistic concerns*. Perfectionistic strivings embody many of the characteristics that come to most people's minds when they think about perfectionism. For example, people with high levels of this form of perfectionism have very high personal standards for themselves. These can include high standards for performance as well as often-unrealistic standards for how long it can take to get something done. When they do happen to meet these standards, they then set their sights on the next goal instead of taking time to savor what they have achieved.

Perfectionistic concerns include many of the same qualities as perfectionistic strivings, but with some very important differences. For people with high levels of this form of perfectionism the standards they set for themselves are almost always unrealistic and beyond what their capabilities or resources can support. This, of course, is essentially a recipe for disaster. By reaching well beyond their current capabilities, these individuals almost ensure that they won't meet the unrealistic goals they set for themselves. As we discuss shortly, it's the aftermath of these failed goals that can be the most damaging both in terms of well-being and how they can fuel procrastination.

Perhaps even more troubling is that people with high perfectionistic concerns are preoccupied with how others view them and their achievements. They believe that others hold them to the high standards they have set for themselves, so if they fail to meet them, then they will not be worthy of love, respect, approval, acceptance, or rewards from other people. They see their worth as being tied to their performance, achievements, and how others view them. Psychologists refer to this as *contingent self-worth*.

Setting unrealistic goals is only one of the reasons why perfectionistic concerns are not considered adaptive by most researchers and clinicians. Equally problematic is the way that this type of perfectionist responds when they encounter the inevitable ups and downs that most of us experience on the road toward reaching our goals.

For people high in perfectionistic concerns, the path toward reaching a goal is expected to be a straight linear upward trajectory, with no "blips" along the way. They expect that not only should their unrealistic goal be reachable but also that the path toward that goal should be perfectly executed. Any signs that their journey is not a smooth, linear route are viewed as indications that they are failing to meet their goal. The problem with this approach is that it assumes that the path to all goals follows a linear path to success, from setting intention, to taking initial action, to reaching the goal (see Figure 6.1).

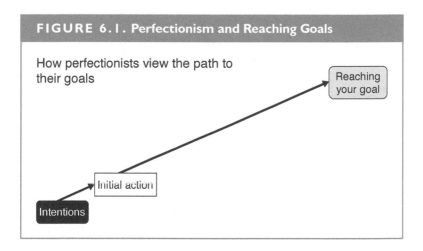

FIGURE 6.1. Perfectionism and Reaching Goals

How perfectionists view the path to their goals

Reaching your goal

Initial action

Intentions

As many of us have experienced, though, the journey to reaching a goal is seldom, if ever, a straight, unhindered beeline to the end, as illustrated in Figure 6.1. Instead, trials and tribulations, unexpected challenges and detours are the natural course for many of the important goals that we pursue. Whether we are trying to get good grades in college, or reaching a healthier weight, or even writing that report for a manager, the journey toward reaching goals can be filled with highs as well as unexpected lows, as depicted in Figure 6.2. These challenges can be viewed as opportunities for personal development and building confidence, if we have the courage to meet them, and sometimes detours and obstacles can set us on a path to our goal that is better than what we could have imagined.

Some people high in perfectionistic concerns view mistakes or lapses that they make on the journey toward their goal as signs that they are not going to be successful. This *zero-tolerance* approach means that they respond negatively to such lapses. Their contingent self-worth kicks in, and they respond with harsh self-criticism and scrutiny as they try to understand why their planned route to their

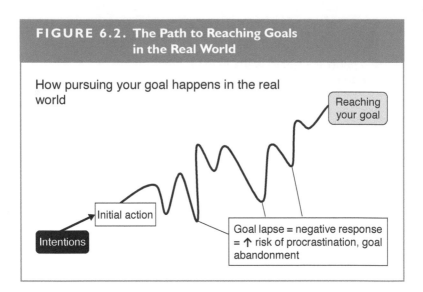

FIGURE 6.2. The Path to Reaching Goals in the Real World

How pursuing your goal happens in the real world

Reaching your goal

Initial action

Intentions

Goal lapse = negative response = ↑ risk of procrastination, goal abandonment

goal is not going as smoothly as planned. This is also why this particular form of perfectionism is often referred to as *self-critical perfectionism*. Moreover, these lapses trigger self-doubts about their ability to reach their goal. It's at these points that the risk for procrastination, or even abandoning the goal altogether, is highest.

Take a Moment

Let's pause again, this time to reflect on your past goal journeys. Think about a recent time when you set and accomplished a goal that unfolded over a period of time. Ask yourself: "Was the path toward reaching my goal smooth?" "Or was it a bit bumpy and challenging, with things not going as expected?" "Or was it a bit of both?" "How did I react when the journey to my goal was bumpier than expected?" "How did I feel toward myself when the journey toward my goal become challenging?"

Why Perfectionism Can Lead to Procrastination

Research that my colleagues and I have conducted supports these ideas and has shown, too, that perfectionistic concerns in particular increase the risk of procrastination (Sirois et al., 2017). We examined, in not just one but 43 different scientific studies conducted by different researchers, which included 10,000 people, how both perfectionistic concerns and perfectionistic strivings are associated with a tendency to procrastinate. Our analyses of these associations, averaged across all the studies, indicated that self-critical perfectionists (i.e., those high in perfectionistic concerns) were more likely to also be prone to procrastination. However, the same was not true for those high in perfectionistic strivings. In fact, those who strove to meet their own personal standards were actually *less* prone to procrastination.

We explained these intriguing findings in terms of how self-critical perfectionists view their chances for success in reaching a goal. Recall that self-regulation involves setting a goal, taking steps to reach the goal, and monitoring whether you are making progress toward the goal. But it also involves estimating what your chances of success will be before you embark on the journey toward the goal. It's at this stage that we take stock of our resources, both those we can call on, such as support from others, time, money and so on, and those we have within ourselves, such as confidence and past experiences.

For people high in perfectionistic concerns, it's at this stage that things can go awry. Self-critical perfectionists view asking for help as a sign they are not doing well and therefore not living up to the perfect performance they believe others expect from them. Much like the shame that people prone to procrastination often experience, self-critical perfectionists are often too ashamed to draw on their social resources to help them with their goals. Now, if you add to this low self-esteem and low confidence in being able to actually accomplish the goal in the perfect way they envision they should, then it becomes clear that they will assess the resources they have to successfully reach their goal as falling short. And if they are concerned that their performance on the task or goal will fall short of their and others' expectations, then not starting it or completing it is a good way to avoid disappointing others and themselves. Consider, for example, the following statement from a student whose perfectionism was preventing them from even getting started on their assignment:

> Despite myself and my best interests, I feel as though everything I write has to come out perfectly in the first draft. This means that I often delay beginning to work on the assignment because I hold unrealistic expectations and desires with regard to my work. I know that procrastination does not help at all, as I will ultimately have less time to accomplish the task at hand, yet I often find myself procrastinating. I feel as though I'm under so much pressure to perform (put on by myself) that it's difficult to even begin doing the task.

These are some of the reasons why self-critical perfectionists may procrastinate even getting started on the journey to their goal. If it can't be perfect, why even try? And if they do happen to get started, once they hit one of the inevitable lapses on their journey their belief that this is a sign they are failing often prompts them to abandon their goal. In either case, the result can be the same: procrastination. But if we can learn to spot when those perfectionistic thoughts are interfering with reaching our goals, and even learn how to set more realistic goals and expectations for our performance, then we can reduce the risk that we will procrastinate and make our journey toward our goal that much more rewarding. As John Quincy Adams once said, "Try and fail, but don't fail to try."

The Unforgiving Path of Self-Criticism
and the Kinder Path of Self-Acceptance

From what we've discussed about low self-esteem and self-critical perfectionism, it is clear that self-criticism can play a large part in feeding some of the negative feelings we can have about ourselves when we are working on our goals. When we doubt our self-worth and expect ourselves to meet impossible standards, we set up a story about ourselves that tears down our confidence about being able to complete our tasks and reach our goal. We might believe that we are not good enough, or worthy enough, or capable enough to accomplish our goals, so why even bother trying? Or we may be hypervigilant to any signs of difficulties while working toward our goals and be quick to judge these as evidence that our negative, judgmental views of ourselves are fact rather than fiction. We blame ourselves rather than circumstances for any deviations on the path to our goal.

This negative, unforgiving internal script of self-blame can quickly become a vicious circle that amplifies those initial negative feelings we had about ourselves and the task. What started as a challenging report we had to write that triggered feelings of self-doubt can spiral into full-blown feelings of anxiety, stress, and dread as our negative self-talk adds fuel to the fire of our negative emotions. With a self-critical mindset and a negative self script, you can get caught up in searching for reasons why things aren't going smoothly, why you are having difficulty executing what you believe should have been a simple task, and why you are having so much trouble simply getting the task done.

If you step back and view self-blame from a functional light, though, a different story emerges. When you blame yourself for the difficulties you experience as you struggle with having an important conversation with a friend, or trying to adopt healthier behaviors, for example, you are trying to explain *why* you are struggling. You are searching for answers to explain why things aren't going the way you expected or hoped, or why something you thought should be easy is so difficult. When you seek the answer to the "why" question, you are trying to gain some sense of control and certainty over a situation over which you may feel out of control.

Blaming ourselves for the difficulties we experience as we grapple with a task is a bit like regaining a sense of control over those difficulties. When we attribute those difficulties to our lack of competence, poor performance, or unworthiness, our feelings of uncertainty about why we are struggling are replaced with certainty and control. Perceiving that we have control over our circumstances can be a powerful stress-buster, and self-blame is like an extreme level of control—we believe that we have control over consequences that are in fact beyond our control. But when we learn to accept that there are always things in life that will be outside of our control, we take the pressure and blame off ourselves. This can help clear the way to focus on the things that really are in our control so that we can take steps to address them.

But although self-blame can restore a sense of control when we are struggling with a task, it does so at a cost. That cost, of course, is the hit our self-esteem takes when we place the burden of blame on our own shoulders rather than looking for external sources of our struggle. If you are struggling with writing a newsletter for your community group because you are unsure what is expected, you could put that down to not having been provided with sufficient information to proceed and ask your group a few questions to clear things up. But if you are someone with low self-esteem, or are a self-critical perfectionist, you'll be more likely to blame your own perceived inadequacies for your struggle. And as numerous research studies have shown, self-blame contributes to feelings of depression, anxiety, and other negative feelings, all of which can make procrastination a convenient coping option.

Take a Moment Follow-Up

Take a look back at the words you used to describe yourself at the beginning of this section. How many of these words were positive descriptors? How many were negative? Take a look at the overall balance of positive to negative descriptors that you used. This can give you clues to the nature of your own self-views and how they might shape your internal scripts and self-talk.

TACKLING THE SOURCE

The key to tackling the source of negative emotions that can prompt an urge to procrastinate is self-awareness. By becoming more aware of the negative emotions you experience when you are struggling with a task, and the negative self-talk that can stoke and maintain these emotions, you can start to diffuse and replace your self-blaming script with one that is supportive. The scripts or stories about yourself that play automatically in your mind when you encounter difficulties are usually underpinned by irrational beliefs.

It's important to also remember that we all have negative scripts that get activated from time to time. Sometimes these scripts are based on false ideas we have developed about ourselves because of what others may have told us (e.g., "It's not good enough") or because of how we have interpreted the outcomes we experienced, often in childhood when a parent wasn't as attentive as we needed them to be (e.g., "She isn't noticing what I did, so I must not be very important"). Once you acknowledge and challenge these beliefs you can then replace them with ones that serve you better and support you as you work toward reaching your goals.

The questions in the "Becoming Aware of How Your Beliefs Shape Your Feelings" exercise aim to help you uncover some of the irrational beliefs that contribute to the negative emotions you experience when you struggle with starting or continuing a task. They are based on principles from cognitive behavior therapy (CBT), a problem-focused approach that aims to help people identify, challenge, and change their thoughts, beliefs, and emotional and behavioral reactions to situations that cause them difficulty. Evidence from several studies indicates that CBT can be an effective approach to help people reduce procrastination (e.g., van Eerde & Klingsieck, 2018).

The questions in this exercise are intended to be a starting point to help you gain insight into the source of some of the negative emotions involved when you are struggling with procrastination. If you wish to go further with this approach, I recommend that you consult a registered CBT psychotherapist for formal CBT sessions. CBT is a focused, short-term therapy that often does not require many sessions to resolve issues.

EXERCISE: Becoming Aware of How Your Beliefs Shape Your Feelings

There are four parts in this exercise, which is designed to help you become more aware of how your beliefs may be fueling negative feelings about yourself when you encounter a difficult or unpleasant task and are tempted to procrastinate. You can complete them in response to a recalled procrastination event or whenever you feel the urge to procrastinate (but not as a form of procrastination, I hope!).

Activating event and consequences for your behavior: Recall a recent time when you procrastinated. Think back to the specifics of the situation or task that prompted you to procrastinate, and describe this briefly below. The sentence stems are to help you get started, but feel free to describe the event in any way that suits you.

EXERCISE: Becoming Aware of How Your Beliefs Shape Your Feelings (*Continued*)

Event	I had to . . .
	(describe the task)
Consequences	Instead, I . . .
	(describe your procrastination)

Beliefs: Recall the thoughts that went through your mind as you struggled with the task. If these don't come easily to mind, then try imagining yourself having to deal with a similar task. What thoughts come quickly to mind? I have added some example beliefs that are quite common when people struggle with tasks that may resonate with you or help you recall your own. Feel free to use these as appropriate and/or add your own.

I'm not _____ enough to finish this task. (*fill in your own adjective[s]*)
If I'm struggling with this task, it means that I am _____ _____. (common responses: "a failure," "not smart," "inadequate," etc.)
If I don't do a good job on this, it means that I _____ _____. (e.g., "won't get promoted," "won't be respected," "will feel ashamed," "will let other people down")
Other people will think that I am _____ if I don't complete this task well.
I can't do this.
Add your own beliefs here:

(continues)

EXERCISE: Becoming Aware of How Your Beliefs Shape Your Feelings (*Continued*)

Dispute: Now that you have identified some of the beliefs that make up your negative script, it's time to challenge these beliefs. What evidence do you have that these beliefs are true? What evidence do you have that these beliefs are distortions and based on half-truths? To help you get started, I've listed some of the common beliefs from the last section here with examples of how they may be disputed.

Your belief	Evidence that disputes this belief
I'm not _____ enough to finish this task.	Challenge these adjectives with objective evidence. If you have advanced training or a university degree, this would dispute, for example, the idea that you are not smart enough.
If I'm struggling with this task, it means that I am _____ _____. If I don't do a good job on this, it means that I _____. Other people will think that I am _____ if I don't complete this task well.	Similar to above, think about evidence that calls into question this belief. If you believe that it means you are a failure, for example, think of all the success you have had in your life that disputes this.
I can't do this.	Think about a time when you completed a similar task. If you've done something like this before, the odds are that you can do it again. Alternatively, think about what information or resources can help you complete this task, and list them here.

EXERCISE: Becoming Aware of How Your Beliefs Shape Your Feelings (*Continued*)

Exchange: Now that you have identified and challenged the beliefs that drive your negative script, it's time to find new, healthier beliefs to replace them. By replacing the old beliefs with new ones that are not distorted, you will be creating a more balanced script to respond to difficult tasks.

Your old belief	Your new replacement belief
I'm not _____ enough to finish this task.	
If I'm struggling with this task, it means that I am _____ _____.	
If I don't do a good job on this, it means that I _____.	
Other people will think that I am _____ if I don't complete this task well.	
I can't do this.	

III

EVIDENCE-BASED STRATEGIES TO HELP YOU STOP PROCRASTINATING

CHAPTER 7

WHY MINDSET MATTERS

It's not what happens to you, but how you react to it that matters.
—Epictetus

In this chapter, you will learn

- why being self-compassionate when you procrastinate can help you get back on track,
- how to become more self-compassionate after you procrastinate,
- why forgiving yourself for procrastination can be motivating, and
- how to know when to use self-compassion or forgiveness to reduce procrastination.

Setting goals and working toward achieving them is no easy task. As you likely have experienced, things don't always go as smoothly as planned. Whether the goal is big or small, there are inevitable ups and downs on the journey toward reaching it. That means that when you do hit that bump in the road, or that unexpected roadblock, or detour, it will likely be unpleasant. You could learn that you don't have the resources or information needed to finish a task or that the task you thought was going to be easy and quick is more difficult and time consuming than you first expected. Or, as I discussed in Chapter 6, the bumps in the road may be of our own making, for example, when we set expectations about our performance that are too high or assume we will not make any mistakes along the way. Regardless of their origin, these unexpected twists and turns can throw you off course and become the fodder that fuels procrastination.

Thankfully, though, this doesn't always have to be the case. Most important is how we react—or, better still, *respond*—to these challenges. Do you see them as signs that you are failing, as indicating there is no chance to accomplish what you want, and thus anticipate the aftermath that will follow in terms of letting yourself and/or others down? Or do you see these ups and downs as a par for the course of any goal? Although challenges are disappointing, perhaps even frustrating, you can learn and possibly even benefit from them. Recall from Chapter 6 that the path toward reaching goals is never a straight, upward trajectory. Ups and downs, highs and lows, are par for the course when pursuing a goal.

A key source of the negative mood that can drive procrastination is the way we view ourselves and our capabilities. Being demotivating, harsh, and unkind to oneself and telling yourself to "just get on with it" can actually backfire and create more of the negative feelings that prompted your procrastination in the first place.

WHY YOUR INTERNAL SCRIPT MATTERS

When trying to achieve your goals, mindset matters. If you have a mindset that includes negative scripts about yourself, then you are more likely to react negatively to any challenges you face when working on your task. The way we view difficulties on the path toward a goal is a reflection of how we see ourselves. Perhaps we believe we are unworthy or not good enough, or we doubt our own capabilities, rather than being self-accepting and reminding ourselves of our strengths. You might expect that anyone else would have an easier time than you are having, or you have a hard time accepting your imperfections and the fact that, like everyone, you can, and do, make mistakes. If this is your attitude, then you will be looking for evidence to support these distorted views of yourself. Any difficulties you might encounter on the journey to completing a task or achieving a goal can then become proof that your doubts and fears are true. In effect, your negative self-views become self-fulfilling and self-reinforcing.

As I noted in Chapter 6, having an internal script that is judgmental, harsh, and unforgiving will make any difficulties you experience while trying to work on your task that much worse. It will add an extra layer of negative feelings to the ones you already have about the task you want to procrastinate. Working to change the irrational beliefs that drive that negative internal script can certainly help but so can learning new ways to respond to any difficulties or lapses you experience while trying to get the task done.

In this chapter, we take an in-depth look at two alternative ways of responding to difficulties that psychological science suggests can reduce distress and increase motivation to persist in the face of obstacles. We explore how and why these approaches can help quiet your inner critic, soothe your picky perfectionist, and defuse the negative emotions and stress that are driving and even maintaining your procrastination. Research has shown that both approaches can reduce procrastination, so you can be confident that responding to your procrastination in these ways will produce results.

You may be surprised to learn that the two approaches I am referring to are *self-compassion* and *forgiveness*. At first glance, these may appear to be unlikely candidates to help reduce procrastination. Being kind and forgiving toward yourself when you are struggling with a challenging task or with your own procrastination could seem like you are letting yourself off the hook, right? It can appear like you are giving yourself a free pass to step away from your responsibility for getting your intended task done and any fallout from doing so. You might feel better, but how will this help you reach your goals?

This is the type of reaction that I commonly get when I tell people that being forgiving and compassionate to yourself can help reduce procrastination. In many ways, though, it's not surprising. We live in a world where many of us have learned that the only way to improve yourself and succeed in life is to push yourself harder and further, to strive to be better, and to accept nothing less than your best. So, if mistakes are made along the journey to a goal, people often believe that the only way to correct these missteps is a swift and often harsh cracking of the whip of self-criticism. This is perfectionism and self-criticism in overdrive, and, as I highlighted in Chapter 6, pursuing your goals this way can take you along a bumpy, difficult path.

The other problem with using self-criticism to motivate one-self is that it often backfires. Self-criticism focuses on the aspects of ourselves and our behaviors that we want to improve. In some circumstances, taking a critical and balanced view of ourselves can be healthy and provide insights that can promote positive changes. For example, if you notice that you tend to procrastinate exercising, you might take a critical view of this issue and discover that you don't like running alone. A healthy response to this insight would lead you to take constructive steps to reduce this tendency by scheduling your runs so that you are with other people.

When taken too far, self-criticism can take on a life of its own. In the example just mentioned, if instead of seeking a running partner you instead did not examine, or accept, why you have difficulty maintaining a regular running routine, and berated yourself for not simply running alone, this response would be less likely to help you get into a running routine. You might start to judge yourself harshly for not being able to run alone. Lots of other people can run alone, so why can't you? This more intense self-criticism can lead to further negative thoughts that generate negative feelings that are demotivating rather than motivating and thus lead to further avoidance.

The solution is to replace these harsh, judgmental, and unforgiving responses with ones that are kind, accepting, and forgiving. This can take some practice, though, because self-criticism and self-blame are often the default responses when we encounter difficulties or lapses while working toward our goals. Thankfully, though, a growing evidence base has documented that both self-compassion and forgiveness can be cultivated as enduring mindsets that can replace our more negative default responses. As we discuss shortly, accepting our difficulties and the negative feelings they cause are central to both of these approaches.

Take a Moment

Let's take a moment to consider your internal scripts. Ask yourself: "What is my usual default response when I make a mistake or do something that I am not proud of, like procrastinating?" "What do I tell myself when this happens?" "Is my internal script accepting and self-soothing, or is it harsh, negative, or self-critical?" "How do I feel after I say these things to myself?" "What effect does this script have on my motivation and confidence to try and correct things and move forward?"

THE BENEFITS OF BEING SELF-COMPASSIONATE WHEN YOU PROCRASTINATE

Most people have a fairly good idea of what it means to be compassionate. If you found out that someone close to you was struggling with their goal, or feeling down because something didn't work out the way they had hoped, you would recognize that they are suffering and be kind and understanding toward them. You would want to console them and make them feel not so alone in their difficulties.

You would be gentle in your words and mindful of not saying anything to add to their suffering. All of these things reflect taking a compassionate response to the difficulties they were experiencing, and would help you support them in trying to make things better. You would certainly not blame them for their difficulties or make them feel like there was something wrong with them because they were struggling.

Being self-compassionate means extending the same compassion to ourselves that we would extend to others. It means having a kind, accepting, and compassionate response to our own difficulties and providing the same understanding and gentle support we would offer to a close friend or family member who was struggling with their own shortcomings and mistakes.

Self-compassion, though, is more than simply showing self-kindness or engaging in self-care. Researcher Kirsten Neff at the University of Texas at Austin views self-compassion as a healthier way of relating to oneself that is grounded in Buddhist psychology (Neff, 2011). From this perspective, being self-compassionate involves three core elements that work together to help people manage the negative emotions and stress they experience after setbacks and struggles or when they notice aspects of themselves that they don't like: (a) responding to ourselves with self-kindness rather than self-criticism, (b) feeling connected rather than isolated in our suffering, and (c) being mindful of our emotions. By being self-compassionate, we support and motivate ourselves to improve and persist with our goals.

What Does Being Self-Compassionate Involve?

The first element of self-compassion involves *responding with self-kindness rather than self-criticism*. When we are self-compassionate, we don't blame ourselves for our difficulties or make negative judgments about ourselves or our character. We don't avoid our feelings about the struggles and challenges we are facing. We don't increase our suffering by holding ourselves to unrealistic expectations or expecting that we should be perfect. Instead, we approach our struggles, inadequacies, and failures with warmth, openness, and acceptance, recognizing that experiencing difficulties and not always getting the outcome we wish for are parts of life.

Consider, for example, Kerry, who is feeling bad about procrastinating making travel arrangements for their family vacation. Kerry was worried about whether everyone would agree with the choice of hotel, car rental, and so on, and now some of the travel costs have gone up because the date for the trip is fast approaching. Responding with self-kindness rather than self-criticism, Kerry might think something along these lines:

> I know that I put this off when I didn't need to, and this may have caused more problems. But I am not going to be hard on myself. I accept that my good intentions to think about others didn't translate into the best outcome this time, and I will do what I can now to make things right.

The second element of self-compassion involves *feeling connected rather than isolated in our suffering*. It involves recognizing that everyone makes mistakes, falls short of what they had hoped for, comes face to face with their own inadequacies and flaws, and suffers as a result. This is all part of being human. Being self-compassionate means acknowledging and accepting these universal truths and feeling connected to others through our suffering. This is one of the key elements of self-compassion that sets it apart from other ways of responding to oneself, such as self-esteem. Self-esteem focuses on evaluating yourself in a positive light; seeing yourself as special; and noting how much you like yourself, often in terms of how you compare to others. Self-compassion isn't about positive evaluations or seeing yourself as better than anyone else. Being compassionate to yourself involves recognizing that you, like everyone else, suffer and deserve compassion.

Often when we make mistakes or have to deal with the aftermath of our inadequacies, we feel isolated and alone in our suffering. We might feel like we are the only one to experience these difficulties and thus may hesitate to share them. We mistakenly believe that other people are doing just fine, are happier than we are, and don't make mistakes or experience failure like us. But this is just an illusion. There is nothing unique about making a mistake or failing. Everyone does it. As John Watson once said, "Be kind; everyone you meet is fighting a hard battle."

Recognizing our common humanity makes it easier to be less judgmental about our mistakes and personal flaws and extend compassion to ourselves. When we accept our common humanity, it is easier to reach out to others for help because we don't fear that we will be judged by them when we reveal our inadequacies and lapses. Research supports this idea and has found that people who are self-compassionate use social support to help them cope with difficulties (e.g., Ewert et al., 2021).

Let's take a look at another example. Tom has been experiencing some new and unusual symptoms that are making it difficult to keep up with his daily responsibilities. Tom has postponed calling his doctor to make an appointment for nearly 2 weeks now because he is afraid of what the diagnosis might be. It's now getting to the point where he sometimes has trouble hiding the pain on his face in his Zoom meetings with friends. One of his friends notices Tom wincing and asks if everything is all right. Instead of trying to hide his discomfort or the fact that he has been putting off seeing the doctor, Tom responds with self-compassion by sharing with his friend what he is going through and openly admitting that he made a mistake by not going to see the doctor when he first noticed the symptoms. His friend is compassionate and says he completely understands. He tells Tom that he too had put off seeing his own doctor for similar reasons in the past, but now he knows why it's important to seek medical help early on, and he encourages Tom to do the same. The next day, Tom calls the doctor to make an appointment.

The third element of self-compassion involves *being mindful of our emotions rather than becoming too invested in and identified with them.* This involves stepping back from our negative emotions and taking a balanced, nonjudgmental view of them and not suppressing or avoiding these emotions or the negative thoughts that stoke them. Being mindful of our emotions also means not exaggerating and becoming immersed in these feelings to the point where we get lost in their momentum and become that anger, frustration, sadness, or distress. We should instead view these emotions with openness, acceptance, and curiosity. Taking a mindful approach to our emotions helps us not overreact to our lapses, mistakes, or personal inadequacies or get stuck in self-pity. When we are engaged in a mindful awareness of our emotions, we can observe them and accept the negative emotions and the suffering we experience from a broader perspective that reminds us that everyone suffers.

What does it look like to be mindful rather than overly identified with our negative emotions? Let's take the example of Jo, who is concerned about her finances, which are a bit tight at the moment. Jo has dreams of saving up to start her own business but is worried that, with all her current expenses, this may never happen. As a result, she has been procrastinating on sitting down and assessing her finances so that she can work out a realistic budget to achieve her goal. After going through her email one day, Jo notices subscription fees that have been charged to her account for months for an online service she no longer uses. These fees add up to a significant amount of money, money that she could have been stashing away to save up for her business. She immediately feels upset and angry with herself for not staying on top of her finances, but rather than becoming absorbed in these feelings she responds to them mindfully. She acknowledges that she is unhappy with her financial procrastination and its fallout and accepts the negative feelings that she is having, rather than avoiding them or becoming too caught up in them. By taking this mindful stance she is then in a better position to be curious as to why she is feeling upset with herself and why she avoided monitoring her finances in the first place. She is also able to see how discovering the unnecessary subscription fees made her aware of the importance of staying in touch with her finances, and this prompted her to check for any other unwanted or unused subscriptions, all of which now put her in a better position to reach her goals.

There is a synergy among the three elements of self-compassion. When we respond to our shortcomings with acceptance and kindness rather than harsh self-criticism, the frustration, disappointment, stress, and other negative emotions that we might otherwise feel are reduced. When we take a balanced and accepting view of the negative emotions we experience after a lapse rather than avoiding them or becoming fused with these feelings, we lay the ground for responding in a gentler way to our difficulties. And remembering that we are not alone in our suffering, and that everyone makes mistakes and fails sometimes, makes it easier to be less judgmental of ourselves and helps us take a more balanced view of our negative emotions, so we can then focus on ways to improve ourselves and reach our goals.

Self-Compassion in Action

So, what do all the components of self-compassion look like in practice? Let's take our example of having to write a report for work. I use this example again not out of convenience but because many people do not enjoy having to write reports for work, especially when there is a lot riding on how well the report is prepared. Recall that the report is due the end of this week and will be used by your manager to make some key decisions. The problem is that you've had this deadline for 2 weeks now but still haven't started working on it. Perhaps you feel unsure about what your manager expects, or you are caught up in thoughts about what will happen if you don't produce a top-notch report, or maybe you simply really dislike writing reports because you have doubts about your writing abilities. Whatever the reason, you have unnecessarily delayed getting started. You've procrastinated.

With this realization, you start to feel bad about yourself. You question why it has taken you so long to get started on such a simple task as writing a report and what is wrong with you. A cascade of other negative thoughts soon follows as you try to understand and gain control over what now feels like an uncontrollable situation. All of this only makes you want to avoid working on the report even more.

What if, instead of this default self-critical script, you have a new, kinder, more self-compassionate script in response to your procrastination? Instead of being self-critical and dwelling on your negative feelings about procrastinating, you accept the fact that you have procrastinated. You remind yourself that being hard on yourself will only make you want to procrastinate more. Instead of denying or avoiding these feelings, or becoming too fixated on them, you acknowledge that you are suffering because you have put things off.

It is important that you also tell yourself that you are not the first person to have procrastinated writing a report, and you won't be the last. But that doesn't mean that you are okay about this lapse. You remind yourself that other people have experienced what you are going through. You tell yourself that even though you're not happy about the fact that you've procrastinated, there is still time to complete the report on time. The report doesn't have to be the best report ever written, it just has to be written and on time. Knowing that others have procrastinated just as you have, you reach out to a colleague for feedback on your ideas for the report. Instead of becoming embroiled in your remorse, stress, and shame over your procrastination, you take constructive, concrete steps to help you reach your goal of writing and completing the report before the deadline. Fast-forward to the end of the week: You have submitted your report to your manager, who is pleased that it is on time. This is what self-compassion looks like in action.

More Self-Compassion = Less Procrastination

You may be thinking at this point that being self-compassionate all sounds fine and well for feeling good about yourself after a lapse or difficulty. But if you're a bit of a skeptic, you might also be wondering how taking a kind and understanding approach to failure or lapses could possibly be helpful when you are trying to reach your goals. Persistence, hard work, and a stiff upper lip in the face of difficulties is the approach that many of us have been told is the best way to achieve goals, right? How can being easy on yourself possibly help when you are fighting an urge to procrastinate or trying to break out of cycle of procrastination?

As counterintuitive as it may sound, scientific evidence has shown that self-compassion can help both reduce procrastination and help people achieve their goals. Consider, for example, a study I conducted a few years back that examined whether people prone to procrastination were self-compassionate and what this meant for their levels of stress (Sirois, 2014b). I asked four groups of people— three groups of students and one group of people from the local community—to complete a survey about how prone they were to procrastination, whether they had a self-compassionate mindset, and their current levels of stress. In each of the four groups, the more prone people were to procrastinating, the less self-compassionate they were. Being less self-compassionate also explained why those who were prone to procrastination reported experiencing higher levels of stress.

This research tells us that people prone to procrastination have a harder time being compassionate toward themselves. In other words, they are more likely to be harshly self-critical, feel isolated in their difficulties, and tend to get consumed by their negative emotions rather than being accepting and mindful of them. This is consistent with many of the ideas that we have been discussing throughout this book. Difficulties managing negative emotions and then also amplifying these emotions with negative self-talk and rumination over mistakes and lapses are the drivers of procrastination.

But we can view this research from a different angle. It also tells us that people who are *less* prone to procrastinate are *more* self-compassionate. In other words, being self-compassionate can be a protective factor against developing a tendency to procrastinate. So, if you procrastinate and respond with self-compassion you will be less likely to continue to procrastinate or engage in ways of thinking that can fuel further procrastination or maintain a procrastination habit. Self-compassion can help defuse the negative feelings and judgments that can make people want to avoid or abandon a challenging task.

More Self-Compassion = More Motivation for Self-Improvement

If we take the above example at face value, self-compassion sounds like the perfect remedy for reducing procrastination and reaching your goals. It provides a healthier, less reactive response to the inevitable difficulties you may experience when pursuing your goals and your urges to procrastinate them. But again, you don't need to simply believe the example I've described above without question. In fact, for a number of reasons that I outline shortly, it's actually better if you question and scrutinize the possible advantages of self-compassion in the light of scientific evidence. Consider what the research says before you decide whether self-compassion can be valuable for achieving your goals.

Consider, for example, a series of studies conducted by Julianna Breines and Serena Chen at the University of California, Berkeley (Breines & Chen, 2012). They set out to test whether being self-compassionate after making a mistake could motivate people to improve themselves. To ensure that their findings were robust and could be applied to different situations, they conducted not one but four different scientific experiments. In each of the experiments the research participants were exposed to, or recalled, a personal failure or shortcoming. These ranged from reflecting on a personal weakness, to recalling a recent time that they did something they regretted or felt ashamed of, to failing a word puzzle task. After each task, some of the participants in each experiment were randomly assigned to a group that was given specific instructions to reflect on their failure or shortcoming with self-compassion. Others were assigned to groups that were either not prompted to respond with self-compassion or were instructed to think about their positive qualities to boost their self-esteem.

The researchers found remarkably consistent results: Across each of the four experiments, participants who took a self-compassionate view of their personal weaknesses reported and demonstrated greater motivation to correct their mistakes and improve themselves than did those who were not instructed to adopt a self-compassionate mindset. For example, those with the self-compassion instructions who performed poorly on a difficult word test that was designed to induce feelings of failure spent more time practicing to try and improve their performance on the second test than the participants who did not receive any instructions to be self-compassionate. In the experiments that involved recalling past failures and weaknesses, those who took a self-compassionate view reported greater motivation to correct their mistakes and work on improving themselves. Together, these experiments provide compelling evidence that self-compassion motivates people to persist in the face of failure and to improve themselves after facing their own shortcomings.

Self-Compassion ≠ Laziness, Self-Indulgence, or Being Irresponsible

I mentioned earlier that it is important to consider the evidence before drawing conclusions about whether and how self-compassion can help you reduce procrastination. The reason I mentioned this was not simply to quell the doubts and questions of your inner skeptic; it was also to draw attention to some important and common misconceptions about self-compassion, namely, that it breeds complacency and laziness, erodes ambition, and hinders achievement. The study I just described is one of many that challenge this faulty view of self-compassion.

The problem is that people don't always understand what being self-compassionate means. They confuse it for self-indulgence, or they think that being accepting of your flaws or failures means that you will give up on trying for better outcomes, not correct mistakes, or neglect self-improvement. At its core, self-compassion involves doing things and treating oneself in ways that are healthy, not harmful. Self-indulgence involves having too much of a good thing to the point where it becomes unhealthy. Eating a whole tub of ice cream to soothe your hurt feelings after a breakup is not being self-compassionate, it's self-indulgent. Acknowledging that you have procrastinated and then telling yourself it is okay, and continuing to procrastinate even though it is costing you your well-being and robbing you of reaching your goals, is not being self-compassionate, it's being complacent and unmotivated.

It turns out that the people who are most likely to hold these misconceptions about self-compassion are those who are not very self-compassionate to begin with. Consider, for example, one study in which the researchers divided participants into two groups: those with high levels of self-compassion and those with low levels of self-compassion (Robinson et al., 2016). They then asked the participants to imagine themselves reacting to a failure, rejection, or loss with self-compassion. Afterward, the participants were asked to rate how they viewed themselves on a series of bipolar adjectives, such as being a success versus a failure, lazy versus industrious, and responsible versus irresponsible. This was done so that the researchers could reveal the beliefs people had about being self-compassionate after things did not go well.

There were some very similar views, as well as striking differences, between how people who were high and low in self-compassion viewed being self-compassionate. Both groups tended to agree that responding with self-compassion to negative events meant experiencing higher levels of well-being. In this respect, their beliefs about the benefits of being self-compassionate to well-being and mental health were aligned with what research has consistently demonstrated.

However, the beliefs held by the two groups about self-compassion diverged when it came to whether self-compassion could enhance performance and goal-related outcomes. Those who were self-compassionate naturally saw self-compassion as an effective strategy for reaching their goals and rated themselves as being ambitious, responsible, and a success. In contrast, those who were low in self-compassion did not see any benefits of self-compassion to achieving their goals. They associated being self-compassionate with being less motivated, less industrious, less ambitious, and irresponsible. These beliefs stand in contrast to what a large number of studies have found to be true: that self-compassion *is* an effective way of helping people reach their goals.

Unfortunately, this research indicates that the very people who would benefit the most from being self-compassionate are also those who are most likely to view self-compassion as something that is detrimental rather than helpful to reaching their goals. I have similarly found in my own research that the beliefs people hold about self-compassion can and do interfere with their ability to learn to be more self-compassionate. For example, in one study my colleagues and I found that instructions to respond with self-compassion to a recent goal lapse were less effective in increasing self-compassion for people who had high levels of perfectionism (Biskas et al., 2022). For those who were not perfectionists, these instructions helped increase their self-compassion and their motivation to pursue rather than abandon their goal. The reason why perfectionists had difficulty being self-compassionate is that they held negative beliefs about what being self-compassionate involves and about the prototypical person who responds with high self-compassion.

The take-away message here is that, yes, self-compassion is a useful strategy for managing the negative feelings we can experience after a lapse, disappointment, or challenge that might otherwise prompt an urge to procrastinate. But it may be a bit more difficult to cultivate a self-compassionate mindset if you hold negative beliefs or doubts about the effectiveness of self-compassion for also bolstering your motivation and ability to persist in the face of difficulties. It's my hope that now that you have been presented with some evidence that disputes these negative beliefs it will be easier for you to try out and put into practice some techniques that have been proven to increase self-compassion and help people cultivate a self-compassionate mindset.

Take a Moment

Let's take a pause and review your own perceptions about being self-compassionate. Ask yourself: "What qualities first come to my mind when I think about someone who is self-compassionate?" "Are these qualities positive or negative or a bit of both?" What if you were now to imagine yourself as someone who was self-compassionate? Ask yourself: "How do I feel being someone who is self-compassionate?" "How easy or difficult is it to imagine myself being self-compassionate?" "Why is that?" As you contemplate your responses, consider how they might relate to the internal scripts that run through your mind when you are struggling with procrastination.

CULTIVATING SELF-COMPASSION

One remarkable thing about self-compassion is that people can learn to cultivate it. There are a number of exercises, meditations, and guided instructions that research has shown can help you begin to view your lapses, shortcomings, and failures from a more self-compassionate perspective rather than defaulting to a harshly self-critical and judgmental response. One of the first steps in learning to be self-compassionate is to become aware of your usual response to difficulties. For example, when you are struggling with a task, what do you tell yourself? Are your thoughts supportive and problem focused, or are they negative, judgmental, and blaming? The exercise at the end of Chapter 6 offers one way to help you become more aware of your internal dialogue and the extent to which you may need to replace it or supplement it with one that is more self-compassionate.

Once you are aware of your default response, you can start to take steps to change it. We started our discussion of self-compassion by highlighting how compassion toward others often comes more easily than compassion toward ourselves. There is an effective technique for learning to be compassionate to yourself when you are struggling with a task and feeling the urge to procrastinate, or feeling bad about your own procrastination, that capitalizes on this. Imagine that it is a good friend, not yourself, who is experiencing the difficulties you are experiencing. How would you respond to this friend? What would you say to support them so that they don't feel so bad about themselves? Write out a couple of lines that express your compassion toward, acceptance of, and support for them. Now read these lines back to yourself.

Reading this more self-compassionate response might feel a bit weird at first, especially if you are someone who is used to a harsher, negative, and judgmental internal script. But if this is the case, then you may want to also question why this is the case. What makes you less deserving of being treated with compassion than a good friend is? The truth is that we are all deserving of compassion. Everyone deserves to be treated with caring and concern when they are suffering, yourself included.

There are a number of more intensive meditation and therapeutic programs, such as the Compassionate Mind Training (P. Gilbert & Procter, 2006), compassion-focused therapy (P. Gilbert, 2009), and the Mindful Self-Compassion program (https://self-compassion.org/the-program/), which were designed to help people cultivate a self-compassionate mindset. Kristen Neff offers a number of self-compassion exercises, including the "How Would You Treat a Friend?" exercise, which builds on the writing exercise we just discussed, as well as guided mediations. All are available for free on her website, https://www.selfcompassion.org.

There is also one approach that my colleagues and I have used for successfully cultivating self-compassion in our research over the past few years. It involves recalling a troubling event and then reframing your responses to the event in a self-compassionate manner, using a set of instructions to guide you (e.g., Sirois, Bogels, et al., 2019). Whether it was

---

EXERCISE: Responding to Your Procrastination With Self-Compassion

1. Think of a recent time when you were struggling with a task that you said you would do and you procrastinated. It could be a task that you started but then you didn't follow through with because you ran into difficulties or doubted your ability to complete it the way you wanted to. Perhaps you delayed starting the task because you found it to be too stressful, or you expected it would be too difficult or time consuming. Recall what happened and how you were feeling in this situation as clearly as you can. Try to vividly imagine yourself back in this situation and what it felt like.

   When this event is clear in your mind, write out a couple of sentences to describe this situation:

   _____

   _____

   _____

2. Thinking about the recent time you procrastinated and wrote about, consider the fact that procrastination is a very common human problem that almost every person has experienced at some point. You're not the first person to procrastinate, and you won't be the last.

   It's also common for people to be hard on themselves when they realize they have procrastinated. But being hard on yourself about your procrastination won't change what happened, and it can actually make things worse. Try instead to take a balanced perspective on your feelings about procrastinating. Be kind, accepting, and compassionate toward yourself about what happened.

   Now write a couple of sentences in the space below expressing this compassion, acceptance, and understanding to yourself about this time you procrastinated, the same way that you would try to support a friend who had gone through something similar.

   _____

   _____

   _____

parents who recalled a troubling parenting event, people who were trying to make healthy changes but had a lapse, or students who had procrastinated, in every experiment in which people were given these instructions, their levels of self-compassion significantly increased, and their negative feelings about the event decreased. When we have compared this exercise with one that simply provides information about the benefits of self-compassion, we have found it is significantly more effective in helping people respond with self-compassion. This highlights an important point about cultivating self-compassion— it is best learned through practice and experience rather than through simply becoming more knowledgeable about self-compassion.

The "Responding to Your Procrastination With Self-Compassion" exercise is best completed in a quiet place where you will be undisturbed. I also recommend that you set aside some time to complete this exercise to get the most out of it. If you find yourself struggling at any point, that's okay. Feel free to step away and try again at another time that may be better for you.

THE PARADOXICAL BENEFITS OF FORGIVENESS FOR PROCRASTINATION

Another strategy that can help reduce procrastination is self-forgiveness. As with self-compassion, most people have some understanding of what forgiveness entails. *Forgiveness* is the voluntary process of letting go of negative feelings such as resentment or anger directed toward another individual or group because of harm they have caused you. This does not mean that you forget what was done, but it does mean that you release the negative emotions you've been holding onto that can be harmful for your own well-being. You accept what happened and move beyond it emotionally.

Self-forgiveness involves showing this same forgiveness to yourself. Like self-compassion, it is often more difficult to forgive yourself than it is to forgive others. When we have done something, such as procrastination, that we know caused harm to ourselves or others, it is easy to fall into the trap of believing that we deserve to be punished for what we did. Being harshly self-critical about what happened can be a form of punishing ourselves that can stand in the way and prevent us from moving beyond our mistakes and learning to self-forgive. Holding on to negative emotions can keep us stuck in the past. When we are consumed with feelings of guilt, shame, and remorse about our procrastination, learning from our mistakes and making amends so that we don't repeat them becomes difficult. When we wallow in these feelings and can't move beyond them, the road to self-forgiveness is blocked.

The Journey of Self-Forgiveness

So, what does the road map to self-forgiveness for procrastination look like? Researchers have proposed that the journey to self-forgiveness involves three key steps (e.g., Wohl et al., 2008). First, you have to *accept that you procrastinated and that you are unhappy with yourself for doing so*. For this to happen, you need to take responsibility for your procrastination. As long as you are blaming your procrastination on outside forces, or not admitting that the delay was voluntary, then you are not truly accepting that you procrastinated. Coming to this realization can be difficult, especially if you are prone to procrastination. Your first instinct will be to avoid anything that brings difficult emotions to the surface. Denial is a wonderfully safe place to be, as they say.

The second step on the journey to forgiving yourself involves *acknowledging and allowing yourself to experience the negative feelings you have about procrastinating*. Again, this is no easy feat if procrastination has become a habit. Are you angry, disappointed, or frustrated with yourself? It's okay to be. As we've been discussing throughout this book, these feelings are completely natural. Feeling bad about procrastinating, whether it's because of your own expectations for yourself or because you're aware that you have transgressed social norms, is a healthy response. But it's what you do with those feelings that makes the difference between improving yourself and reaching your goals versus getting stuck in a vicious circle of wallowing in shame, guilt, and other distressing emotions that perpetuates the very behavior that you feel bad about in the first place.

Once you have fully acknowledged your negative feelings about procrastinating, then you are ready for the last and final step to self-forgiveness—*overcoming those feelings*. This part of the journey involves working through and coming to terms with your negative feelings about procrastinating, without ruminating about them. It means that you have to accept what you did and forgive yourself and that you must stop punishing yourself and focus instead on making amends. In other words, you have to shift from a *retribution* mindset to a *restitution* mindset. Ask yourself what you can do so that you will be less likely to make the mistake of procrastinating again. Then take action to change your behavior.

More Self-Forgiveness = Less Procrastination

Here again, you might be thinking that using self-forgiveness as a strategy to help reduce procrastination goes against common sense. As I have just outlined, feeling bad about procrastinating is a common and reasonable response. On the surface, it would appear that if you forgive yourself for procrastinating, then you are wiping out any motivation to make changes because you feel guilty about procrastinating. But consider that negative emotions, when left unchecked, can drive you to procrastinate further rather than motivate you to stop it. So, if forgiving yourself makes you feel less guilty and ashamed about procrastinating, then this should, in principle, reduce future procrastination.

What does the evidence say about using self-forgiveness to address procrastination? In one very clever study, researchers at Carleton University in Canada tested whether self-forgiveness could reduce procrastination among university students who were studying for exams (Wohl et al., 2010). The students completed questions about the extent to which they had procrastinated studying for an upcoming exam and whether they forgave themselves for their procrastination. Because the researchers also wanted to see whether self-forgiveness predicted later procrastination, they had the students complete these questions twice, once before their first midterm exam and then again before their second midterm, which was after they had received their first exam grade. The students also reported their mood after receiving their exam grade.

The results were both paradoxical and encouraging. Students who forgave themselves for procrastinating while preparing for the first exam were less likely to procrastinate on preparing for the second exam, and the reason they procrastinated less came down to mood: Those who practiced self-forgiveness experienced less negative mood, which in turn reduced their procrastination. In contrast, the students who did not forgive themselves for procrastinating on the first exam felt worse about their performance and continued to procrastinate their studying for the second exam. This research tells us that self-forgiveness provides an effective means of regulating negative mood that leads to approaching and dealing with problems rather than avoiding them by procrastinating.

Thankfully, self-forgiveness, like self-compassion, is something that can be cultivated with practice. The "Forgiving Yourself for Procrastinating" exercise will provide you with guidance on how to start to forgive yourself for your procrastination.

EXERCISE: Forgiving Yourself for Procrastinating

Often after we procrastinate, we have negative feelings toward ourselves that we can't easily let go of. Do you find yourself saying any of the following after you procrastinate?

"I dislike myself for procrastinating"
"I criticize myself because of my procrastination"
"I put myself down because of my tendency to procrastinate"

If you answered "yes" to any of these, then it may be time to practice some self-forgiveness. When you forgive yourself for something you did, even if you did it to yourself (such as procrastination), it releases these negative feelings and allows you to rechannel your thoughts to help restore a more positive view of yourself.

The following steps can help you reach self-forgiveness:

1. **Take responsibility, but don't self-blame:** Acknowledge and accept that you procrastinated and that this was harmful to you. Accept that your delay was unnecessary and not due to external forces. This is the first step on the journey to self-forgiveness. But it's also important to not indulge in self-blame. Responsibility means being accountable and in doing so discovering ways to take actions to repair the problems your procrastination created. Self-blame, on the other hand, continues a downward spiral of negative, critical thoughts and fear that can be on constant replay and take you back down the road of procrastination.
   Tell yourself:

   a. "I accept that I procrastinated"
   b. "I take responsibility for any harm caused by my procrastination"
   c. "I am accountable for my procrastination"

   Note how it feels as you say these statements to yourself. Is it easy or difficult to believe what you are telling yourself? If you are having difficulty with these statements, you may find it helpful to write out your thoughts to explore the reasons why.

(continues)

2. **Acknowledge how you feel, with gentleness and compassion:** Own your negative feelings about your procrastination rather than ignoring or avoiding them. Acknowledging these feelings allows you to feel remorse, which can pave the way toward making amends and progressing with your task. But it's also important to do this with a generous spirit and compassion. Remind yourself that you, like every other person, are worthy of forgiveness.

   Tell yourself:

   a. "I feel _____ that I procrastinated"
   b. "As I consider that procrastinating was wrong, I feel accepting toward myself"
   c. "I accept that I procrastinated, and I am compassionate toward myself"
   d. "I am worthy of forgiveness"

   Again, note how you feel after saying these statements to yourself. Do you experience any resistance to acknowledging these statements as being true for you?

3. **Shift from retribution to restitution and restoration:** Once you have worked through your negative feelings and release any feelings of self-blame, it will be easier to refocus and start to see how to move forward and feel better about yourself. You will be able to release the ghosts of your procrastination so that they do not haunt you and use up the resources that you need to get back on track with your task.

   Ask yourself the following questions:

   a. "What possible insights, and opportunities for self-improvement, can I learn from procrastinating?"
   b. "What can I do now to make amends for the problems created by my procrastination?"
   c. "What can I do so that I lessen the chances that I will procrastinate on this task again?"

   As you start to restore a more positive view of yourself, it will become easier to take steps to rectify the problems from your procrastination. In doing so, you will learn that mistakes can be fixed and that the insights from these mistakes can help you improve yourself.

SELF-COMPASSION VERSUS SELF-FORGIVENESS: WHICH ONE WHEN?

Self-compassion and self-forgiveness are two evidence-based responses to difficulties that can help promote self-acceptance. They both are effective for dispelling the negative and distressing emotions that can drive you to procrastinate and even maintain a procrastination habit. But there are also some important distinctions between them that can help you choose which is best for certain circumstances.

For example, when you are struggling with a task, have made a mistake, and are feeling frustrated or stressed and on the brink of procrastinating, self-compassion will be more useful than self-forgiveness. Why? Because you haven't actually procrastinated yet. Self-forgiveness requires a transgression to be committed before you can forgive yourself. Now, that doesn't mean that you have to wait until your struggle with the task goes that far before you can respond in a healthier way—quite the contrary. The negative emotions and thoughts that are brewing as you struggle with the task can be managed by making a self-compassionate response to them. By being compassionate to your own suffering, you can lessen these feelings, accept your struggle, and increase your motivation to complete your task.

When you are feeling distressed because you have already procrastinated, responding with either self-forgiveness or self-compassion can be effective to ensure you don't continue to procrastinate. Self-forgiveness may be especially appropriate when the task you have procrastinated has significant implications for yourself or other people. Let's say that you procrastinated filing your tax return and that your partner could not file theirs until you did. This unnecessary delay has potential negative financial consequences for both you and your partner. You would feel a lot worse if your procrastination has consequences that are so concrete or that harmed others.

Self-forgiveness would help you come to terms with the consequences of your procrastination, allowing you to put it behind you and focus on making amends rather than punishing yourself about it.

When the aftermath of your procrastination is less concrete or less harmful to others, but still distressing to you, self-compassion is the balm to soothe your suffering and motivate you to get back on track. It can help short-circuit any tendency to ruminate about your procrastination that can fuel further procrastination. Responding with self-compassion provides you with a balanced and connected perspective that helps you feel more motivated to move forward and reduce your procrastination.

CHAPTER 8

PERSPECTIVE MATTERS: THE POWER OF REFRAMING

Your reality is as you perceive it to be. So it is true, that by altering this perception we can alter our reality.
—William Constantine

In this chapter, you will learn

- why your predictions about how you feel about a task can be faulty,
- how to focus on the journey of your goal to help reduce procrastination,
- why focusing on the inner rewards you gain from your task can reduce procrastination, and
- how to find the *why* of your goals to make them more meaningful.

Perspective is a powerful tool. How we frame a particular situation that we encounter invariably affects the way we respond to it. Recall that in Chapter 6 we delved into the sources of the negative mood that can prompt procrastination. People tend to put off tasks that are unpleasant and aversive, and whether we view a task as aversive or not often depends on the stage of the project. But rather than simply blaming our mood on the task, we also took a closer look at the internal sources that can make certain tasks seem more or less aversive. Low self-esteem, unhealthy perfectionism, and self-blaming tendencies were identified as key culprits in stirring up negative reactions to the inevitable difficulties we face when working toward our goals, often making emotional mountains out of molehills.

One thing that each of these negative ways of relating to oneself has in common is how they can color the way we view our goals and any challenges we face when trying to achieve them. If you are a perfectionist, then achieving goals and completing tasks without incident are badges of self-worth, whereas any signs of trouble spell certain defeat. If you are someone with low self-esteem, difficulties are signs that you are incompetent and a failure. And if you are prone to self-blame and encounter problems on the road to achieving your goal, then these bumps in the road are seen as evidence that you did something wrong.

But when you swap out the lens of negative self-evaluation for one that is kinder, accepting, and forgiving, everything changes. In Chapter 7, we explored how responding to ourselves when we were struggling with a task and our procrastination in a gentler way can lead to vastly different outcomes. Instead of generating even more negative emotions about yourself and the task you are struggling with, being compassionate and forgiving of yourself can transform negative feelings and distress. Seeing yourself through this new lens provides an opportunity to come to terms with this distress, rather than wallowing in it or avoiding it, and transforms these feelings into a call for action to improve yourself and your behavior so that you are less likely to procrastinate in the future. In short, perspective matters when it comes to tackling procrastination.

In this chapter, we continue to address the importance of perspective when addressing procrastination. We explore how changing the way we view a task is also an important strategy to manage our feelings and to make that hedonic shift from negative to positive mood without having to procrastinate to do so. That unpleasant conversation with a friend or coworker you must have, that small but nagging home repair project you can never seem to get around to, or that challenging goal to start eating healthier and exercising more are examples of goals that can trigger unpleasant feelings and an urge to procrastinate. In psychological terms, these tasks are stimuli: the things we encounter in our environment that provoke reactions such as distress, frustration, anxiety, and so on. When we procrastinate, we avoid both the stimuli and the negative emotions that they trigger.

But what if you were to change the stimuli—or, more specifically, how you see these tasks? When we change how we view the stimulus (the task), then the emotions that are triggered in response to that stimulus also will change. To accomplish this, you need to use strategies that will help you reframe tasks that are at first glance unpleasant or anxiety provoking in ways that will shine a light on the opportunities they can provide you. Although this isn't always something that comes naturally for everyone, it fortunately is a skill that can be learned through practicing focus-shifting strategies and techniques.

In the next sections, I present and unpack a number of different techniques and strategies that research suggests are effective for reframing procrastinated tasks. I discuss three main types of strategies: (a) addressing biases, (b) focusing on the "how" of your goal, and (c) finding and making meaning. These evidence-based approaches can help shift your perspective of the task from something that is threatening or unpleasant to something that is meaningful and manageable. Instead of being something that you are dreading and avoiding, the task can become something that you look forward to doing.

DON'T ENTRUST YOUR EMOTIONS TO A CRYSTAL BALL

Think about the last time you were struggling with an unpleasant task. Perhaps you were having trouble getting started, or maybe you started it but encountered a difficulty you hadn't anticipated. If you are like most people, you probably began to think about just how difficult the task was going to be and how you would feel while you were trying to work through the challenges that you anticipated this task would pose. And if you expected that you would find it very frustrating or stressful to work through these difficulties, you were likely tempted to procrastinate, or perhaps you even gave in and did procrastinate.

Predictions such as these that people make about their future emotional states are referred to by psychologists as *affective forecasting*. When facing decisions about choices and courses of action, people often rely heavily on their ability to forecast how they will feel in the future. So, if you anticipate that a task is going to be unpleasant or frustrating, or that resolving a difficult part of the task will be particularly stressful for you, your forecast of those emotional experiences could be negative enough to prompt you to procrastinate. This forward thinking is just good planning though, right? Well, according to the scientific evidence, not quite.

Research has repeatedly shown that people are actually not very accurate in predicting how they will feel about certain events in the future. When we use a "psychological crystal ball" to try to peek at our future emotional states, our conclusions are, more often than not, faulty. We can usually distinguish between whether we will have positive or negative feelings about an upcoming event. For example, you might anticipate the positive feelings you would experience when you meet up with a childhood friend or the negative feelings that you would have if you fail or do poorly on an exam or test. But where we tend to be much less accurate is when we try to estimate how long we will experience these feelings and how intensely we will experience them. In short, our estimates of how we will feel in the future are more often biased than not.

When we try to use our psychological crystal ball to predict how we will feel in the future, two psychological biases can creep in and distort our perspective. I don't mean far future predictions, such as how you will feel years from now. These biases come into play *any* time we mentally time travel to a moment in the future that is not in the present moment and try to imagine how we will feel then.

Future Emotions Are Less Intense and Don't Last as Long as We Expect

One reason why we are not very good at predicting how we will feel in the future is because we tend to overestimate the intensity of the feelings we expect to experience. If you are applying for a job promotion, the actual level of happiness you experience when you get that much-anticipated phone call will usually pale in comparison to your expectations for how happy you will be if you get it. Likewise, if you anticipate that you will feel very bad if you do poorly on a test or assignment, how bad you actually feel will usually be much less intense than what you predicted when you find out your grade. We psychologists refer to this as the *intensity bias*.

A good illustration of this bias at work comes from a study conducted by researchers at Wilfred Laurier University in Canada (Buehler & McFarland, 2001). They asked students who were expecting the results from an exam to rate how they would feel if they received grades that were above what they expected or below what they expected. The students then rated how they actually felt, literally the moment after they received their results. Those who received a negative outcome on the exam expected that they would feel much worse than they actually did when they saw their results. But that's not all: The students made their predictions less than an hour before they received their exam results. This is a great example not only of how the emotions we anticipate we will feel are much more powerful than what they actually are but also of how this bias comes into play even for predictions in the immediate future.

Another bias that can make us inaccurately estimate our future emotional states involves a tendency to overestimate how long we will experience emotions in the future. When people are anticipating a negative outcome, such as a failed exam or rejected job application, they tend to expect that their emotional experience will last much longer than it actually does. This is referred to as the *durability bias*. In essence, people overestimate how enduring their emotional states connected to an event will be. Numerous studies have demonstrated that people tend to expect their negative states to persist well beyond what they actually do.

Consider, for example, a study that was conducted with people who were about to take their driving test. Researchers from the City University of London asked would-be drivers at a test center to answer questions about their current and anticipated levels of happiness minutes before their test, right after their test, and then 1 week later (Ayton et al., 2007). Not surprisingly, when asked before learning their test results, those who actually failed their driving test had predicted that they would not feel very happy about failing. What was surprising, though, was how they actually felt 1 week later: Those who failed the test rated their actual happiness 1 week later much higher than what they had anticipated. In essence, they expected that they would still feel the same disappointment 1 week later as they did immediately after learning of their failure.

Remember Your Emotional Immune System

One of the reasons people experience these biases when estimating their emotional states is that they often underestimate, or even ignore, the role of their internal coping resources in helping them to adjust (D. T. Gilbert et al., 1998). When we experience adversity or challenges, we mobilize different resources to help us cope with difficulties and dial down our negative emotions. So, for example, if you've just received bad news that you didn't get that job you wanted, you may try to reframe this negative event in way that will be less threatening and distressing so as to reduce both its emotional impact and how long this impact lasts. But because we are usually not fully aware of these coping processes, we don't take them into account when we predict how we will feel should we experience difficulties. This leads us to overestimate both how bad we will feel and how long those negative feelings will last. Psychologists have referred to this coping response as our *emotional immune system* because it operates automatically and beneath our awareness to help speed up emotional recovery from troubling events (D. T. Gilbert et al., 1998).

These biases also come into play when we try to anticipate how we will feel about a task that we need to complete. As you can imagine, most times we overestimate how frustrating, distressing, and unpleasant a task is going to be, often before we have even started it. For example, your perceptions of working on balancing your monthly budget so that you can reach your financial goals can transform from being mildly unpleasant to downright stressful. The problem is that your faulty predictions about exactly how bad you will feel if you attempt to work on your budget often become just another reason to procrastinate that task to avoid those feelings.

How do you overcome these biases so that they don't drive you to make faulty predictions that fuel procrastination? Well, becoming more aware of these biases and how and why they work, as you just have, can certainly help. But, like any preconception, these affective forecasting biases operate automatically, which means they can kick in and exaggerate your negative feelings about a task quite quickly. Before you know it, you've already decided to procrastinate as a way to avoid what you expect you will feel.

There is another solution. Several studies have found that when people focus on an unpleasant or challenging event in isolation, their predicted emotions are much more intense than when they consider this same event in light of their past experiences (e.g., Ayton et al., 2007). In other words, focusing on how you felt when you dealt with similar challenges in the past can shine a light on other factors that affect your emotional reactions. This can then help reduce the biases that will lead you to believe that you will feel a lot worse, for a lot longer, than what may actually be the case.

What this all means in terms of reducing procrastination is that, in most cases, your psychological crystal ball is not very accurate. How you expect to feel as you work on that unpleasant task is not likely to match how you actually will feel. People often overestimate how intense emotional experiences will be and how long they will last. But if you step back and remind yourself of how you felt when you grappled with a similar task in the past, you can defuse these biases and reframe your expected emotional experiences in a more realistic way. From this perspective, it will be easier to find a way to manage those emotions that doesn't involve procrastinating.

Take a Moment

Let's pause. Ask yourself: "What task am I procrastinating right now?" "How is it similar to another task I've dealt with in the past?" "How did I feel when I procrastinated last time?" "How intensely did I feel that way, and for how long?" "What coping skills did I use to help me manage those feelings?"

IT'S ABOUT THE JOURNEY, NOT THE DESTINATION

Often when we think about goals we think about the outcome. We wonder if we will be successful in reaching our goal. But more than this, we also think about what reaching our goal means. Whether your goal is to find a new job, get down to a healthier weight, or learn a new language so your overseas trip will be more enjoyable, you focus on the outcome of the goal and how far or close you are from reaching it.

Setting and staying focused on your goal is an important part of self-regulation. "Keep your eyes on the prize" is a common motivational saying when people are struggling to reach a goal. However, being solely focused on the outcome of reaching your goal can come at a cost if it's exclusive to a consideration of other important perspectives. For example, focusing too much on reaching your goal can trigger fears about *not* reaching the goal and what this might mean. You might compare how far away you are in relation to where you need to be or would like to be. If you have to write a 50-page report and you have written only five pages, then focusing on the outcome can be discouraging and cause self-doubt and negative internal scripts to rise to the surface. All of this can undermine your confidence and feed an urge to procrastinate.

Fear of failure is also more likely to rear its ugly head when you have a rigid focus on the outcome. Fear of not succeeding is a well-known contributor to procrastination, and it plays a prominent role in perfectionism. As we discussed in Chapter 6, perfectionism can make you more vigilant to any sign that you won't achieve the outcome you want. Lapses and detours on the road to your goal are seen as signs of failure rather than part of the natural course of goal pursuit. And if you have convinced yourself that your efforts are going nowhere and that you will fail to write that report on time, or to a standard that you are happy with, then why bother trying, right? Viewed from this perspective, procrastination seems an inevitable outcome, or at least one that is more likely than success.

However, we can also view our goals from another perspective. Goals unfold over time. Achieving a goal is not simply a question of setting one and then reaching it. Setting off to reach our goal is like embarking on a journey. On many journeys there are detours, side roads, diversions, and other unexpected twists and turns along the way. When you reframe your goal as a journey rather than an outcome, the process of reaching the goal comes to the forefront.

The focus becomes what you can learn along the way, rather than simply what you gain when you reach the end. From this perspective, simply engaging with the goal can become a goal in itself. The means becomes the end. The inevitable ups and downs during goal pursuit become part of the passing scenery rather than signposts that you are heading for failure.

Take Time to Savor Your Goal Journey

A focus on the process of reaching the goal has other benefits that can help you successfully navigate the ups and downs of the journey. Focusing on the goal journey rather than the goal destination makes it easier to see the individual steps needed to accomplish the goal. It's the difference between focusing only on getting from Point A to Point B on a map versus making an effort to enjoy all the small towns and villages you pass through along the way. If you stay on the highway and focus only on reaching your destination city, your trip will likely be very long and boring. But if you take time to take in the sights along the way, the trip will be that much more enjoyable.

Viewing our goal as being composed of smaller, more concrete subgoals (the towns and villages in the metaphor above) can make it seem more manageable and less threatening than viewing it as one large task that can seem overwhelming. When we see a task as overwhelming, we feel stressed, and when we feel stressed about a task we are more likely to procrastinate it. Consider, for example, this situation that one woman found herself in when planning her wedding:

> I procrastinated on looking at venues for my wedding next year. I wanted to get it booked and sorted but felt like it was such a big task and big decision that I kept putting it off. It made me feel bad and feel a constant nagging in the back of my mind to get it done, but I ignored it for weeks.

In this example, she viewed booking a wedding venue as a huge task that prompted her to procrastinate it. Taking a process-oriented view of this important goal would have let her break it down into smaller tasks, such as making a list of possible venues, setting up viewing appointments, making a cost and benefit list for each venue, and so on. Each of these smaller tasks would feel much more manageable and have made it less likely that she would procrastinate. By taking a process-oriented view she would have also had an opportunity to enjoy each step on this journey toward her wedding day, rather than stressing about the end result.

This is one of the key differences between focusing on the process versus the outcome of a goal. Viewing goals as a journey provides opportunities to find meaning and enjoyment that can counteract any urges to procrastinate. You can view a goal as an adventure that may lead you to new discoveries about yourself. You might develop your strengths and learn new skills as you work through the necessary but sometimes challenging steps toward your goal. Simply being engaged with the goal can take the focus off your concerns or fears about whether or not you will reach the goal.

The *How* Versus the *What* of Pursuing Your Goals

What you focus on when you are pursuing your goal matters. If you want to reduce your risk for procrastination, is it better to focus on the journey, the *how* you get from start to finish? Or is it best to focus on the destination, *what* you want to achieve?

These are the very questions that researchers at the University of Zurich set out to answer in a study of people working toward exercise goals (Kaftan & Freund, 2020). The researchers specifically targeted people wanting to start a new high-intensity interval training (HIIT) program, a form of exercise that has become increasingly popular. After receiving initial instructions from a fitness trainer, the participants were sent home with a link to the HIIT exercise routine they had committed to engage with four times a week at specific times, over an 8-week period. This was an ideal setup to examine possible procrastination of the exercise routines because it was something all participants said they wanted to do, and they were left to their own devices to follow through or not.

The researchers tracked participants' progress carefully to understand whether or not they were procrastinating. For example, they asked the participants to complete regular questionnaires about whether they were successful in following the exercise program and whether and when they procrastinated their workout routines. But they also asked participants questions about their mood, their intentions to exercise versus procrastinate, and the extent to which they were focusing on the (a) workout itself (a focus on process) and (b) what they wanted to achieve by working out (a focus on outcome). At the end of the study, everyone also reported whether they thought they had successfully reached their exercise goals.

What the researchers found painted a fairly clear picture of which type of focus was better for achieving goals and reducing the risk of procrastination. Across the 8 weeks of the study, focusing more on the process of working out—for example, enjoying working out for its own sake—translated into greater success in completing the workouts and better performance. Focusing on the outcome of the workouts—for example, getting more fit—did not predict success or performance. Moreover, on days when people focused on the process of their workout they expressed fewer intentions to procrastinate. On such days they also saw their workout as being less difficult and more enjoyable, and they felt more satisfied with their workout and confident that they would be successful in completing the entire exercise program.

Focusing on the outcome of the workout had none of these benefits. In fact, when people focused on the outcome of the exercise program, they saw their workout as more difficult, and they had stronger intentions to continue to procrastinate if they had already procrastinated a planned workout. In short, focusing on the workout itself was adaptive; it led to better success, greater well-being, and less procrastination. Focusing on what the workout would lead to in the end was not adaptive.

Now, rather than jumping to the conclusion that we should avoid focusing on the outcome, know that the researchers also uncovered some evidence that occasionally focusing on the outcome could be beneficial. When participants focused on the outcome of their exercise workouts, they saw them as being important and felt more motivated to continue. This makes sense if we consider the value of sometimes stepping back and reconnecting with the larger reasons why we engage in goals in the first place. So, for example, if you remind yourself that you are doing these incredibly challenging HIIT workouts because you want to become more fit and lose weight, then this may help keep you motivated, especially if you are having a particularly tough day. In such instances, connecting the *how* of the workouts to the larger *why* you are doing them can make the workouts seem more meaningful. And, as we discuss in the next section of this chapter, meaning making can be a very powerful tool to combat procrastination.

The take-away message here is that shifting your perspective to focus more on the journey you take in reaching your goal, rather than only the outcome, can be an effective strategy and reduce your chances of procrastination. Although it's important to actually set a clear goal and have that outcome in mind when you want to accomplish something, too much of a focus on that outcome can bring with it fears about not being successful. More than that, constantly focusing on the outcome can rob you of opportunities to experience the steps along the journey to your goal and the enjoyment and confidence that doing so brings.

Take a Moment

Let's pause here. Imagine that you have to go to the doctor for a colonoscopy or another test or screening that isn't very pleasant. Just thinking about this makes you feel uncomfortable and ready to ignore the inevitable reminder phone calls about your appointment. What if, instead of thinking about the destination (the unpleasant test), you thought about the journey, so you plan to make this journey to a somewhat unpleasant destination more enjoyable. For example, you invite a friend to join you who has had this test before. Not only can they help allay your fears, but having them accompany you also gives you a chance to catch up with them and find out how they are doing. Your friend also helps you remember *why* you are getting the test done. Getting this test will be a way of being kind to yourself now as well as protecting the health of your Future Self so that Future You can enjoy playing with your (future) children or grandchildren. After the test, you stop by your favorite coffee shop to unwind with your friend. What started as an unpleasant destination has become simply a pit stop on an enjoyable journey of renewed friendship and a confirmation of your commitment to your current and future health.

MEANING, LOST AND FOUND

In an ideal world, we would be able to pick and choose the tasks that we want to do, and that we find enjoyable, and leave the rest behind. You could become deeply engaged in doing the things that bring you joy, energize you, and stimulate your curiosity and your mind. In such a world it would be easy to think that procrastination doesn't exist. If there were no reason to do things you would rather avoid then you would never have to find ways to manage your feelings of uncertainty, or frustration, or boredom by procrastinating. In this ideal world of only enjoyable tasks, you wouldn't be reading this book—there would have been no reason for me to write it.

However, there's a problem with this picture. It assumes that when we are engaged in tasks that we enjoy doing, and are working toward goals that we are excited about, we will never encounter any problems or obstacles. But in this perfect world of doing only your favorite things, would it really be the case that you would *never* encounter difficulties or frustrations or ever be bored? Probably not.

Human beings have a wonderful capacity to adapt quite quickly and skillfully to their environments. It's this capacity that has allowed our species to survive as long as it has, through numerous life-threatening disasters, both natural and human-made. This capacity to swiftly adapt to our circumstances is reflected in our physiology through the various mechanisms of homeostasis that help keep our internal systems in balance when outer circumstances change. But it is also reflected in our psychological processes. Recall, for example, the psychological immune system I noted earlier in this chapter that helps us cope with negative outcomes by helping us reframe negative situations in such a way that our emotional reactions are less extreme.

Beyond coping with negative situations, there are psychological processes that help us adapt even when the events we are experiencing are enjoyable and pleasant. One of these processes is *habituation*. Because we are exposed to so much information every day, our psychological systems have evolved processes to help us manage this information without becoming overwhelmed. If we are exposed repeatedly to something in our environment, we learn to selectively ignore it over time so that our limited attentional resources aren't taxed. This process helps us to adapt to negative circumstances so that they are not so alarming or stressful each time.

But habituation doesn't discriminate between positive and negative experiences. Any stimuli or experience can become less negative or less positive if it repeats over time. Consider, for example, biting into a delicious piece of your favorite food. Research has found that the initial bite is much more pleasurable than the third or the tenth bite that you take. This habituation to positive and negative experiences is referred to by psychologists as the *hedonic treadmill*. In essence, when we experience intense or heightened periods of positive emotions and happiness we eventually adapt and settle back down to our average level of these emotions, what is often referred to as our *set point*. For example, most lottery winners are initially ecstatic but within a year are no happier than they were before they won the lottery. Researchers have estimated that although about 60% of this set point is determined by genetics and the environment we are raised in, the remaining portion is influenced by other factors, including what we do and how we think (e.g., Lyubomirsky et al., 2005).

Giving in When Feeling Less Good

If we return to our thought experiment about a world in which you have to do only the things you really enjoy, it should be pretty clear that at some point your positive emotions will fade. It's also very likely that they will be replaced by other, less pleasant, emotions if you happen to run into a slowdown, unexpected problem, or if you simply start to get bored. But the point of this thought experiment was not to discourage; instead, I wanted to highlight the fact that even when we are doing things that are enjoyable it takes work to overcome the natural process of hedonic adaptation to habituate to those pleasurable feelings. We have to actively remind ourselves why they are enjoyable; otherwise, we will become accustomed to them, and the positive feelings that we get from the task soon fade. It's at these moments that we are at risk for procrastination, especially if there is another task that might offer more promise for enjoyment.

This is exactly what my team and I have found in our research. A colleague and I conducted two studies to examine how people's levels of positive feelings toward a task are involved in procrastination (Sirois & Giguère, 2018). One study involved students working on academic tasks whom we tracked over a 2-day period, and the other included people from the community who wanted to make healthy lifestyle changes over the next 6 months. In both studies, we asked our participants about how they felt about their goal initially and at a follow-up. But we also asked them the extent to which they experienced social temptations while they were working on their goals. Some of the social temptations included invitations to go to parties instead of studying and requests to indulge in unhealthy foods instead of sticking to a diet.

We found that having negative feelings, such as frustration, toward the task was not the only factor that predicted procrastination at the follow-up. Participants who experienced less enjoyment of their task over the study period were also more likely to procrastinate. This was especially true if they were already prone to procrastination. More important, though, is that feeling less positive about the task, and the impact of this on procrastination, were amplified if they were exposed to social temptations. In other words, simply having an alternative and more pleasurable activity made the enjoyment of the task they were working on pale in comparison. This could be due in part to habituation: The novelty of the social activities would certainly make them appear to initially be more enjoyable than the planned goals. And when the participants felt less enjoyment, they were more likely to procrastinate on their goal.

But even when we are engaged in a task or goal that is pleasurable and meaningful to us, we might still be tempted to procrastinate. To manage this risk, we need to find ways to connect with the meaning of the task. We need to ask ourselves some deeper questions. Why is this task important to complete? What will achieving this goal will mean to me? Yes, this does mean focusing on the outcome of the goal. But it's exactly in these circumstances, when your interest in and enjoyment of your task are waning, that putting the outcome in the spotlight can be beneficial for reenergizing your motivation so that you can get back to enjoying the process of engaging with your goal.

There is no shortage of research studies that attest to the power of meaningfulness as a motivator and source of positive emotions (e.g., Heintzelman & King, 2014). Reconnecting with the meaning-fulness of our tasks and goals can counteract hedonic adaptation as well as buffer us from social and other temptations that can make the goal or task on which we are working seem less enjoyable or impor-tant. Tasks that give us a sense of purpose, connection to others, enjoyment, and that strengthen our sense of identity are experienced as meaningful, and, as the discussion up to this point has made clear, we are less likely to procrastinate when or goal is meaningful to us.

What happens, though, when you have to do something that is less than meaningful to begin with? You may find that you have committed to tasks and goals that lack enjoyment and don't feel worthwhile to you. They may be tasks that you felt obliged to say "yes" to but in which you have very little real interest. Perhaps you have taken on a task because of the rewards you will get from others, such as money, praise, and so on, which don't necessarily speak to your deeper personal needs.

Take a Moment

Let's pause to consider the tasks that you find less meaningful and may want to procrastinate. Ask yourself: "Is there a task that I have committed to that I feel that I *have* to do?" "Do I find this task less meaningful?" But what if, instead of thinking about this task as something that is not as much in your control and that you *have to* do, you thought of it as something that you *get to* do? This simple substitution of "get to" for "have to" can help shift your perspective from one of obligation to opportunity. When you see even small tasks as opportunities—perhaps to demonstrate or hone your skills, develop greater self-confidence, or show someone you care—you can feel more grateful for these tasks and infuse them with greater meaning.

Is Your Task Motivated by Internal or External Rewards?

If you find yourself struggling to find meaning in a task, your motivations are the likely culprit. Psychologists commonly view motivation as falling along a continuum ranging from being driven by external rewards (*extrinsic motivation*) to being driven by internal rewards (*intrinsic motivation*). When you are motivated by extrinsic rewards it can feel like someone else is in the driver's seat. You let other people determine whether and what rewards you will receive for your efforts, as well as the punishments if you fail to meet your goal. You have to conform to what others want you to do rather than determining your own behavior and choices. This is also referred to as *controlled motivation* because you can sense that your actions are controlled by outside forces and standards rather than by your own needs and values. When you are extrinsically motivated, acquiring wealth, fame, and being attractive tend to be key themes that underpin your goals.

But when your main reason for engaging in a task or goal is because you find it enjoyable, interesting, and satisfying, then your motivations are intrinsic—the rewards come from within. This type of motivation is autonomous and resides at the other end of the spectrum. You make choices and act in a self-determined manner rather than relying on others to use the proverbial carrot and stick to guide your behavior. When your goals are intrinsically motivated, the focus is on personal development, mastery, and connecting with others. Your goals become meaningful because they are aligned with your core values and needs. By engaging with these goals, you feel that you are the author of your own destiny.

As you may have already guessed, when your goals are primarily self-motivated and autonomous rather than controlled, it is less likely that you will procrastinate. This is in part because you find such goals more enjoyable and satisfying and thus less aversive. In the research I discussed in Chapter 6 involving how people felt about the different stages of their projects, when people saw their tasks as autonomous they also rated them as being more personally meaningful and less unpleasant.

There are other benefits to viewing a goal as something that you initiate and over which you have control that can reduce procrastination. Seeing your task from this more meaningful standpoint changes your perspective on any difficulties you experience on the journey toward completion. Slowdowns can become opportunities to reconnect with the bigger "why" of your goal and reinstate your commitment to seeing things through.

Difficulties and challenges can also provide a chance to use your inner resources and learn more about your capabilities and limits, two activities that are essential for personal development. When you view difficulties from this lens of meaning, any feelings of frustration or discouragement that you experience can be harnessed to motivate, rather than hinder, persistence to reach your goal. From this perspective, procrastination is simply not an option.

All of this should make clear that finding meaning in goals and tasks is important for enjoying them more and procrastinating them less. Of course, it helps if you initially choose goals that are driven by intrinsic values rather than the external rewards they will bring. It is much easier to find meaning in intrinsically motivated tasks than in those you have taken on primarily for extrinsic reasons.

How to Find Meaning in Your Goals

Even with goals that appear to be focused more on external than internal rewards, it's often the case that there is a seed of intrinsic value if we look hard enough and ask the right questions. Going back to our example of having to write a report for your manager because you want to impress her and help your application for promotion (extrinsic motivations), you could also step back and see that your efforts in striving to write an excellent report are helping you develop into a better report writer (intrinsic motivation). By writing this report you are gaining valuable experience that you can carry forward when you write your next report. From this perspective, even if your report isn't as spectacular as you hoped it would be, you have still gained something from engaging with this goal.

There are other ways to find or add meaning to goals for which your intrinsic motivations are low and the urge to procrastinate high. Consider, for example, a goal that many of us often have: starting a new exercise routine. Becoming more physically fit takes effort, especially when we are trying to get into new routines and overcome the inertia of old habits. Sometimes the reason for getting more fit stems from extrinsic reasons, such as wanting to be more attractive or because our peers are more fit than we are. The immediate benefits to ourselves may not always be clear, especially as we struggle with the aches and pains of using muscles we didn't even know we had.

Fortunately, there's a surprisingly easy way to almost instantly add meaning to goals like this. Find something else that you do enjoy doing and tether it to your goal. So, for example, if you are struggling getting a new exercise routine started, and you enjoy social contact, invite a friend to join you on your runs or workout routines. This will make working toward your goal not only more enjoyable but also more meaningful. Spending more time with a friend can help you learn more about each other and deepen your connection. And on those days when you feel less than inspired to go for a run, your friend will be there to support you and remind you why procrastinating your fitness goal isn't in your best interest.

Another way to help find meaning in your goals and ward off urges to procrastinate is to take stock of the meaning of these goals. This involves thinking first about a goal for which your motivation may be waning or for which you have encountered difficulties and setbacks that are making procrastination a tempting option. From there, ask yourself one or more questions to help dig beneath the surface and determine the deeper reasons why the goal or task is important to you. I've included an exercise at the end of this chapter ("Finding the *Why* of Your Goals") to guide you on your journey toward discovering the meanings of your goals.

You may be wondering if this exercise is just something that I put together on the basis of the ideas I've been discussing and whether it will really work to reduce procrastination. At least, this is a question I would ask if I were reading this. Although the exercise is grounded in the principles of motivation science, it is also one my colleagues and I have scientifically tested and found hard evidence to indicate that it does work to increase meaning and reduce procrastination.

One of my former PhD students, Sisi Yang, designed and conducted a very clever experiment that used a version of this exercise to determine whether helping people find the meaning in their goals could help them lower their chance of procrastinating (Yang et al., 2021). She recruited people to participate in her study who were working on a goal to be completed over the coming week and asked them to complete questions about their tendency to procrastinate, their mood, and the meaningfulness of their goal. Next, she randomly assigned them to one of three groups—meaning making, positive emotions, and control—each with a different set of instructions for writing about their goal. Participants in the meaning-making group received an instruction set similar to the one in the "Finding the *Why* of Your Goals" exercise. The positive emotions group completed a similar set of instructions that focused instead on the positive feelings they had about the task. Participants in the control group were asked to write about a neutral event that had happened to them that day; this was to ensure that any changes observed were not simply due to the act of writing about the goal. After this, the participants also reported their current mood and the meaningfulness of their goal. They were contacted 3 to 4 days later and asked to report the amount of time they had spent procrastinating their goal.

Not surprisingly, those who were prone to procrastination rated their goals as being less meaningful at the outset and had more negative and fewer positive feelings toward their goal. But the more exciting finding had to do with the effect these instructions had on actual procrastination behavior. Not only did answering the questions about goal meaning increase the meaningfulness of the goals for this group relative to the other two groups, but those who completed the goal-meaning exercise reported that they spent less time procrastinating relative to the control group. In fact, the people in the meaning-making group procrastinated, on average, 2 hours less than those who received the neutral writing instructions. Moreover, Sisi found that the reason why the meaning-making instructions worked was because they helped decrease people's negative emotions about their goal. To top it all off, her results remained consistent even after she took into account whether people had tendencies to procrastinate. This means that this exercise is effective not only for people prone to procrastination but also for anyone who may be on the brink of procrastinating.

The take-away message here is simple but by no means trivial: Meaning making can help reduce procrastination. Whether it's tethering unpleasant tasks to those that are more enjoyable, reminding yourself of the intrinsic reasons why you are doing what you are doing, or probing the values underlying your goal, making your goals more meaningful and less unpleasant is a solid, evidence-based strategy that can help you procrastinate less.

EXERCISE: Finding the *Why* of Your Goals

We all have goals from time to time that we start to feel less enthused about and that we may be tempted to procrastinate. We may question why we are doing them at all, especially if we reach an impasse and become frustrated or discouraged.

This exercise will help you probe the meaning of these goals so that you can find, or rediscover, the bigger reasons why you are pursuing them.

Start by listing one goal or task that you are struggling with now and that you may be at risk for procrastinating: _____

_____

Now take some time to think about the meaningful aspects of your goal, that is, the ways in which your goal has value for you and gives you a sense of purpose. Use one or more of the following statements to help you focus on the more meaningful aspects of your goal.

Write as much as you can about the personal meaning of your goal. Aim to write at least one to two sentences per statement.

1. Completing this goal will be valuable to how I see myself, because

_____

_____

_____

2. Completing this goal will be valuable to how I connect to others, because

_____

_____

_____

3. Completing this goal will be valuable to my personal growth, because

_____

_____

_____

CHAPTER 9

EMBRACE YOUR FUTURE SELF TO BRIDGE THE TEMPORAL GAP

Do something today that your future self will thank you for.
—Sean Patrick Flanery

In this chapter, you will learn

- how reducing the emotional gaps between your Present Self and Future Self can reduce procrastination,
- why taking the perspective of your Future Self can make it harder to procrastinate, and
- how to have a conversation with your Future Self to feel more inspired and motivated to accomplish your goals.

We all mentally time travel. Whether it's reminiscing nostalgically about warm memories from your childhood or thinking ahead to what your life might be like when you land that perfect job or travel to your favorite vacation destination, mentally traveling to times other than the present moment is a common habit. In fact, we are the only species on this planet that has this incredible capacity to mentally simulate other temporal landscapes and place ourselves within them. Stepping into our own mental time travel machines to visit past and future selves is a normal, healthy function of human consciousness.

This capacity can certainly have some benefits, especially when it comes to conceiving of and achieving our goals. When planning our goals, we might think back to the past to see what did and didn't work so that we use better strategies and avoid making the same mistakes. More important, though, we need to look to the future and imagine the steps along the journey to our goal as well as what our life will be like when we reach our goal. This is why thinking about the future is an essential part of pursuing goals.

But again, you don't need to simply take my word for it—listen to what the research has to say. In a study led by one of my former PhD students, Harriet Baird, we gathered and analyzed all the available research on how different time perspectives were associated with the different processes involved in self-regulation (Baird et al., 2021). A person's *time perspective* can be thought of as the predominant time frame they use when they make decisions. Time perspective is something we develop across our different experiences and what we learn from those experiences. For example, if you repeatedly find that focusing on the future gives you the rewards that you value, then this gives you more reasons to focus on the future next time you have a decision to make. If, however, you find that focusing on the future when you make decisions leads to problems, then it's likely that you will be less inclined to consider the future next time you have to make a decision.

Now, going back to our study, we analyzed not only how having a future time perspective was linked to self-regulation but also how past and present time perspectives were involved. Overall, we analyzed 378 studies that tested how time perspective was linked to all the stages of self-regulation—from setting goals, to monitoring goals, to taking steps to reach goals, and, finally, achieving goals. The message from the results was loud and clear: Having a future time perspective was linked to *better* goal setting and goal monitoring; a higher likelihood of taking action; and better outcomes in health, academic performance, career, and other important areas of life. On the other hand, having a present time perspective was linked to *worse* self-regulation and outcomes.

This research tells us that a lack of focus on the future is a hallmark of poor self-regulation. This shouldn't be surprising in light of what we discussed in Chapter 5 about how difficulties thinking about the future can promote procrastination. When we procrastinate, the future feels more abstract and less concrete than the very real set of negative emotions, or lack of positive emotions, that we experience in the present as we struggle with a task. So we make a temporal trade-off. We prioritize making a hedonic shift in our emotions in the present over taking steps to accomplish our goals in the future.

This raises the question of whether it's better to reduce our focus on the present or increase our focus on the future to effectively reduce procrastination—or is a combination of the two the best strategy? In this chapter, we explore these questions and the intriguing answers revealed by psychological science. We examine some simple yet effective techniques to help you foster a better and more empathic relationship between your Future Self and your Present Self. Once you are on better terms with you Future Self, you'll find that it will be a lot harder to procrastinate.

MIND THE TEMPORAL GAP

When we set out to accomplish a task or reach a goal, we are trying to bridge a gap between what is and what can be. We start with where we are in the present moment, with an intention to complete a task or reach a goal. But embedded within that intention is a glimpse of the future, a future that includes our completed task or goal.

When we set an intention to do something, we are not simply imagining what that task or goal will look like when we accomplish it in the future. On some levels we are also imagining how we will feel when we have completed our task. In essence, we are simulating what it will feel like to be *that* future self, that temporal version of ourselves that will almost certainly exist after a certain amount of time has passed.

So, if it takes a week to complete your task, then it is the 1-week Future You that you are imagining sitting happily satisfied that the newsletter was completed on time, for example. If it's a larger goal, then it may be your 6-month or even 1-year Future You whom you are envisioning when you reach the end of the journey and achieve your goal. In short, when you want to finish a task or reach a goal, you are trying to bridge the gap between your Present and Future Self. You want your Present Self to be sitting in that happy, satisfied place where you believe your Future Self will be when the intended task has been accomplished. But, as has been said on many a road trip, we are not there yet.

This gap between the Present and Future Self creates a temporal tension that can make you feel uneasy. This uneasiness comes from being aware of the discrepancy between where and who you currently are and where and who you would like to be. This isn't necessarily a bad thing; in fact, numerous studies have shown that awareness of this gap can generate negative feelings that have motivational value (e.g., Phillips & Silvia, 2005). These negative feelings of frustration, anxiety, or stress can spur people to make the effort to reduce the discrepancy between their current and ideal Future Self. In short, when we experience this negative mood we want to close the gap so we can feel better, so we work toward accomplishing our task or goal. In this way, the discomfort we experience from this gap can fuel persistence, at least for some people.

The issue is that taking steps to close such a gap isn't the only way to manage temporal tension between the Future and Present Self. There's another, simpler solution we can default to. We can also avoid the negative feelings that arise from this tension by taking one of the players out of the equation. If you avoid thinking about your future, aka your intention to follow through with your task, then you are also avoiding thinking about your Future Self. A consequence of this is that there is no longer any tension with your Present Self:

problem solved. With your Future Self out of the picture, you can focus on ways to make your Present Self feel good now and be free of the uncomfortable or unpleasant feelings that come from being reminded of your unfinished task. When we procrastinate we are in effect avoiding our Future Self.

Avoiding the Future or Fixated on the Present?

At this point you might be questioning whether procrastination is more an issue of not thinking about the future or thinking too exclusively about the present. Perhaps it's a bit of both. This is an important question to ask because the answer can direct us to the most effective strategies to reduce our procrastination. To better manage procrastination, should we try to focus more on connecting with the Future Self, or should we take some of the emphasis off our Present Self?

These are the very questions I wanted to answer when I conducted a study on how chronic procrastination is linked to future and present time perspectives (Sirois, 2014a). But because I wanted to be confident in what I found, I looked at these relationships in not just one study, but in all the published and unpublished research that had examined chronic procrastination and time perspective. This amounted to 14 studies that included data from more than 4,300 people.

I found that in every single study a tendency to procrastinate was associated with being less apt to think about the future when making decisions. I calculated the average of these associations and noted that the overall size was moderately strong. For having a present time perspective, though, the results were less consistent and strong. Being prone to procrastination was linked to being more inclined to think about the present but only in some of the studies. Also, in contrast to what I found in regard to having a future time perspective, the average size of the association of procrastination with having a present time perspective was modest at best. This tells us that the lion's share of responsibility for procrastination falls on thinking *less* about the future. Thinking only about the present plays a relatively minor role and is more likely a by-product of avoiding putting the spotlight on how your actions and decisions will affect your Future Self. And as I outlined earlier, there are good reasons to avoid thinking about your Future Self, especially if managing negative emotions is something you struggle with.

Negotiating this temporal gap without stirring up feelings that will trigger avoidance and, of course, procrastination, can present quite a conundrum. But that doesn't mean there aren't strategies that can help. The trick involves not viewing your Future Self as someone who is distant and abstract.

Closing the Gap Between Your Present and Future Self

As discussed in Chapter 5, we have a natural tendency to see our Future Self more like a stranger than a friend. This is due in part to the abstract nature of the future, especially the far future. But it also has to do with our tendency to equate temporal distance with psychological and emotional distance. A Future Self who feels far away in time will also feel more unlike the person you are today, that is, your Present Self. This can make it easy to expect that your Future Self will have somehow changed in dramatic ways, making it easier to fantasize that they can handle the things you can't bring yourself to do today.

The following experience described by a research participant is a good example of how this can play out:

> I procrastinated with a task I had to perform at work around two weeks ago. It was a task that I was unsure how successful the outcome would be due to my lack of experience with the tools I had to use. I feel if I "put off" doing something that I feel I will struggle with or will feel negative about during the task

there is a chance that in between now and starting the task I will
have gained something that will make the task easier.

This individual believed that somehow they would have "gained
something"—likely new knowledge or new skills—if they waited and
put their task off to their Future Self. The problem is that the degree
of change we expect will happen rarely does, because we are still the
same person we were when we put the task off. We often use this type
of belief to rationalize our unnecessary delay and justify making our
Future Self our beast of burden.

So, how can you close this apparent gap between your Present
and Future Self? William James, arguably the father of Western psychology, suggested that despite being aware that we have different
selves that exist over time, we also have a "consciousness of personal
sameness." This consciousness helps us see the connections between
our temporal selves that exist in the past, present, and future, uniting
them as one sense of self. So, when you picture yourself enjoying
summer vacation last year or imagine what your vacation will be like
this coming year, you know that these images are of temporal versions
of yourself and not someone else. When we recognize this sense of
self-continuity, the gaps between Present and Future Self are mini-
mized and, as a result, so is their potential to provoke procrastination.

Do you remember making or seeing paper people chains? You
took a piece of paper and folded it and then cut out the outline of
a person on one of the sides. When you expanded these folds, you
would get a chain of identical people holding hands. You can think
of your different temporal selves as being connected in much the
same way. Each self is just a different version of your current self,
only further down the chain in time. But when you focus only on
the Future Self who is at the end of the chain, the Future Self who
has reached the goal or finished the task, then you can lose sight of
what connects you to that Future Self. This can make that self feel

more distant and less like the person you are now. As illustrated in Figure 9.1, this can make the temporal gap between your Present and Future Self seem like a canyon.

But what if instead of focusing only on the Future Self who will be there at the finish line you also focus on all those intermediate Future Selves who link you to that end game Future Self? The temporal tension eases. The gaps between each of these intermediate temporal selves is far less noticeable. As a result, you feel more connected and closer to your various Future Selves than disconnected and distant from them. This can also make it harder to make decisions and choices that your Future Self will pay the price for, such as procrastinating.

Consider, for example, a newsletter you have to write for your community group that is due in a week. If you focus on your concerns about how you can write a good newsletter—the end result— then that thought alone can make your 1-week Future Self seem very distant. The temporal gap widens. Your end-game Future Self seems more abstract than real as a result, and your concern for their welfare also weakens. If you give in to these worries, then you may be tempted to put off starting the newsletter so you can feel better now. After all, there is still lots of time, and Future you will be more than capable of writing that newsletter.

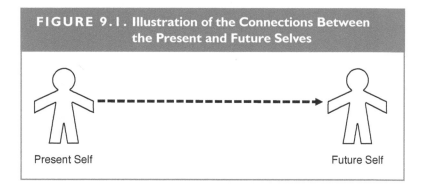

FIGURE 9.1. Illustration of the Connections Between the Present and Future Selves

Present Self

Future Self

Now, instead of focusing on the outcome and your 1-week Future Self, what if you focused on your immediate Future Self—the Future Self of tomorrow? This Future Self is going to feel psychologically and emotionally closer and more real than your 1-week Future Self. So, if you were to procrastinate starting the newsletter, you'd have a fairly good idea of how you would feel tomorrow—more stressed, and likely not very happy with your Past, now–Present Self. But if you were to at least get started today on the newsletter, then the Future You of tomorrow would feel a lot better and have a clearer idea of what needs to be done next. This temporal relationship between a hypothetical Present Self and Future Self is depicted in Figure 9.2.

When tomorrow arrives, that now–Present Self can then take the same approach to thinking about what needs to be done and get on with it, keeping in mind the welfare of the next Future Self of tomorrow. By focusing on these close connections to your near Future Selves, and not just the more distant, end-game Future Self, you take the spotlight off the larger temporal gap and all the negative feelings that come with it. The gaps are smaller, the negative feelings are more manageable, and you can experience a greater sense of continuity and compassion for all of your temporal selves.

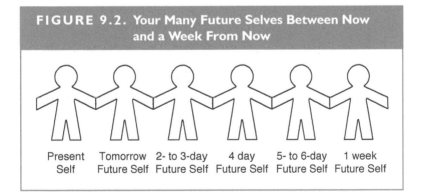

FIGURE 9.2. Your Many Future Selves Between Now and a Week From Now

| Present Self | Tomorrow Future Self | 2- to 3-day Future Self | 4 day Future Self | 5- to 6-day Future Self | 1 week Future Self |

Research that I and others have conducted supports these ideas. When people are asked to rate how close or distant they feel to Future Selves that will exist at different points in time, the Future Self in 1 week is rated as feeling psychologically closer and more real than a Future Self that will exist in 1 month or 1 year. This pattern holds for most people, except those who are more self-compassionate. I have found, across several studies, that people for whom being self-compassionate comes easy feel closer to their Future Self as their Future Self gets further away in time (e.g., Sirois, 2016). It's as if people who are self-compassionate don't differentiate between their different temporal selves—it's all just Self to them, regardless of what space in time that Self occupies. And because self-compassionate people are less likely to procrastinate, taking a more inclusive and connected approach to our temporal selves can be a useful strategy to reduce procrastination.

The take-away message here is that if you want to curb a tendency to procrastinate, the best strategy is to *not* make distinctions between your different temporal selves. They are all versions of yourself traveling through time, learning from experiences, and doing the best that they can so that Present You can reach your goals and get your tasks completed on time. Doing what you can today with what you have to make progress on your goals is one of the best ways you can show compassion to your Present and various Future Selves.

Take a Moment

It's time for a pause. Ask yourself: "When was the last time I thought about my Future Self?" "How hard or easy was it to think about my Future Self?" "Did my Future Self feel emotionally close and like a good friend, or did Future me feel distant like a stranger?"

WALK A MILE IN YOUR FUTURE SELF'S SHOES

In addition to mentally time traveling, perspective-taking is another wonderful and uniquely human capacity. Each of us sees and experiences life through our own unique lens. The same event can happen to us and someone else, and yet what we take away from this event will be unique to us. If, for example, you and your friend apply for the same job, and neither of you are asked to interview, you might see this as a sign that the job wasn't a good fit for you. Your friend, on the other hand, may take it far more personally and have their confidence shaken. Both of these worldviews are valid. But if you simply tried to get your friend to see this outcome the same way you do, then you would miss an opportunity deepen your relationship with them and feel more connected. You wouldn't have the chance to listen to and learn about their struggles over the past year as they tried to find a suitable job or how much they had their heart set on this particular job.

Missing such opportunities is understandable. Because we know our own perspective best, it's easy to slip into thinking that others will see things the same way we do. This assumption, however, is seldom true. If we want to understand what others are going through and how they experience events, we need to put our own narrow view of reality aside and be willing respect other perspectives. When we take the perspective of another person we not only see things through their eyes, but we also understand how they experience and understand the world. By taking their perspective, we develop empathy and compassion for them instead of imposing our own lens of reality onto their circumstances.

Now, perspective taking is most often considered in reference to the perspective of other people. But what if the "other" perspective you took was that of your Future Self? What if you could see your future through the eyes of your Future Self? Would that change how close you felt to that Future Self? Would doing so make you less likely to procrastinate?

These intriguing questions were the basis of an ingenious study conducted by researchers at Carleton University in Canada (Blouin-Hudon & Pychyl, 2017). They wanted to see whether perspective taking could be used as a strategy to foster a closer and more empathic bond with the Future Self. If it did, then would this reduce how much people procrastinated? To answer this question, the researchers designed a mental imagery audio exercise that instructed undergraduate students to mentally time travel to vividly imagine their Future Self and take the perspective of this Future Self.

Taking the perspective of another person can be done in two ways. We can observe what the other person is doing from a third-person perspective, as if we are watching them like we would a character in a movie. From this perspective, we can see the space that person is in and what they are doing, to get a more general overview of their experiences. However, we can also take a first-person perspective. This is the perspective you take, for example, when you are playing a video game and you experience everything from the eyes of that character. From this perspective you literally step into the other person's shoes and imagine what it is like to be them. You experience specific sensations, such as sights, smells, and sounds, as well as emotions that you imagine they would feel in that situation.

Imagining another's experiences from a first- or third-person perspective can be effective in creating a closer connection with that individual, but there are some important distinctions, too. Research has shown, for example, that when we take a first-person perspective and focus on concrete experiences we also feel stronger and more intense emotions from that person's point of view. This can increase our sense of empathy and compassion for that individual. In contrast, when we take a third-person perspective the emotional experiences we imagine are less intense. We tend instead to see their experiences in broader strokes that give us an overall perspective on what situations are like for that person, but without the emotional intensity.

The researchers wanted the student participants to re-create an accurate, dynamic simulation of their Future Self so that they could get a better empathic understanding of and connection with that Future Self. To do this, they instructed the students to start with a third-person perspective of their Future Self and then move to a first-person perspective.

For example, after having the students take a few deep breaths, close their eyes, and relax, the audio instructions told them to imagine their Future Self at the end of the semester, standing a few feet away from them. They then were instructed to notice the space they were in, including the lighting conditions, the time of day, and any furniture. From here they were asked to imagine their Future Self with a textbook, along with details about the desk it was on, what the computer screen looked like, and so on, and to focus on their Future Self's feelings and facial expressions.

Next, the participants were told to shift to a first-person perspective, to imagine what it was like to be actually inside the body of their end-of-semester Future Self, to feel the breath coming in and out of the lungs of their Future Self, to look at their hands, and to listen to any sound made as they picked up books. The students imagined themselves as their Future Self engaged with other academic tasks, such as reading and answering emails, writing in a notebook, and so on. But they were also asked to consider how prepared their Future Self felt for the upcoming exam period and whether they felt as prepared as they would like to be or if they had put things off.

To test whether their perspective-taking exercise was effective, the researchers needed to compare it with a similar task that might be relaxing but that didn't involve the Future Self. They chose a simple relaxing audio meditation. The students were asked to focus on their breathing and the present moment. The researchers randomly chose half of the students to receive this relaxing focus-on-the-present mental imagery exercise and the other half to receive the Future Self perspective-taking exercise. Both groups were asked to listen to their audio exercise twice a week for a 4-week period and to complete measures of perspective taking, empathy, and the degree to which they felt close to their Future Self. They also were asked about how much they had procrastinated over the 4-week period.

What did they find? As you might expect, compared with the students who only took part in the relaxation meditation, the students who mentally time traveled to meet and take the perspective of their end-of-semester Future Self reported feeling more connected to that Future Self. But it wasn't simply that they felt closer; they also experienced more empathy for their Future Self. Seeing what their Future Self saw, and how they felt at the end of the term, gave them a greater understanding of what life would be like for the future versions of themselves. If their Future Self was stressed because work had been put off, then they had a more vivid, first-hand experience of what this would be like. More important, those who had put themselves in the shoes of the Future Self also reported that their procrastination decreased over the 4 weeks of the study.

If we translate this research into a practical message for reducing procrastination, then vividly imagining and empathically engaging with your Future Self will make that Future Self feel more real and less abstract to you. That Future Self will feel more like a good friend whom you want to respect and less like a stranger whom you might ignore. When you can move beyond seeing your situation only from the perspective of your Present Self and consider seeing it from the perspective of your Future Self, you will be less likely to do things that will harm that temporal version of yourself that exists in the future.

When you take this broader temporal perspective of yourself, it is easier to think of your own welfare and be compassionate toward yourself and thus to not procrastinate.

HAVE A CONVERSATION WITH YOUR FUTURE SELF

Focusing on more immediate Future Selves and mentally time traveling to take the perspective of your Future Self are two tactics that can help you reduce procrastination. These strategies help close the temporal and psychological gap between your Present and Future Selves and in turn can help you empathically embrace your Future Self as someone who is real and worthy of your consideration.

Mental imagery is one way you can take the perspective of your Future Self and reap the benefits of this better connection, but it's not the only way to close the temporal gap and improve that felt connection. Any activity that helps you identify and engage with your Future Self in a concrete manner can serve to forge a connection over time.

One technique that has shown some promise for forging closer ties with a Future Self is writing a letter to your Future Self. This exercise is fairly straightforward: You write the letter to an imagined Future Self about anything you like, as if you were having a discussion with them. In fact, this technique is based on a therapeutic technique from Gestalt psychology called the *empty chair technique*; it is an approach designed to help people gain a deeper understanding of another person's perspective. Clients sit in one chair, across from an empty chair, and then have a conversation with the empty chair, even moving over to sit in the empty chair to role play what they think the other person will say. As strange as it sounds, this technique of having a dialogue with your Future Self, whether through role playing or by letter, has some support for improving the connection to that Future Self (Chishima & Wilson, 2020).

Which Future Self Should You Have a Conversation With?

But *which* Future Self you have the conversation with does matter. As research has shown and we have discussed previously, if the Future Self is too far in the future they will feel abstract and too distant. This can highlight that breadth of the temporal gap between you and them and raise uncomfortable feelings, as well as make them feel too much like a stranger. If the Future Self is not far enough away in time, then it may be difficult to see them as being different from who you are today, and any motivational edge for changing your current behaviors will be lost. The trick is to choose that "sweet spot" in time that is just far enough away without being too far.

Whether a Future Self is too far or too close is also relative to the task or goal at hand. An ideal Future Self is one whose success with a goal depends on actions you do or do not take today. Consider, for example a study conducted by researchers at Wilfred Laurier University, who examined whether writing to a Future Self would help high school students feel closer to their Future Self and improve their study behaviors and performance (Chishima & Wilson, 2020). The researchers chose the 3-year Future Self for the students to focus on because this would align with when the students had graduated and were embarking on their career paths.

Instead of using a simple write-a-letter-to-your-Future Self exercise, the researchers added in another important element. Before the students wrote the letter to their 3-year Future Self they were asked to create an imaginary but realistic profile of their Future Self, detailing what their life was like, their occupation, relationships, residence, and so on. After they had created this profile, they wrote the letter to their Future Self.

To make this exercise even more like the empty chair technique, the researchers also had the students write back to their Present Self from the perspective of their Future Self. The students were told to review the profile they had created for their Future Self and then imagine themselves as this 3-year Future Self when they wrote their reply. The intent was to help students close the loop between their Present and Future Selves and more closely simulate a real dialogue.

The results showed that this simple letter writing exercise worked: After writing a letter to their Future Self, and replying back, students felt closer and more connected to their Future Self. What these results didn't reveal, however, was whether it was necessary to write both the initial letter and the reply. Would one round of letter writing have been sufficient to draw the students closer to their Future Self? What are the downstream consequences, if any, of becoming more connected to a Future Self using this technique?

To answer these important questions, the researchers conducted a second study using the same technique, but this time they divided the students into two groups: one in which they wrote a letter and replied to the Future Self as the participants in the first study and one in which they wrote only the initial letter, without a reply. The researchers also checked in with the students after 1 month to see whether their feelings of being more connected to their Future Self had changed. They also wanted to know whether there had been any impact on the students' career planning activities and their ability to resist temptations to procrastinate on their academic work.

They found that yes, engaging in a back-and-forth exchange with the Future Self was important. To get the best results, it was necessary to send a letter to a Future Self and to reply back as that Future Self. The students who wrote to their Future Self and replied from the perspective of that Future Self felt significantly closer to their Future Self after 1 month than did the students who wrote only once. More important, the students who engaged in an exchange with their Future Self also reported more career planning and were better able to resist procrastinating on their academic work. In short, the back-and-forth letter writing technique was the most effective in bridging the temporal gap and reducing procrastination.

Dear Future Self . . .

How can you put into practice this simple yet effective technique? As you may have already gathered, this approach seems to work best for longer range goals. If the goal or task has too short of a temporal time frame, then there isn't enough tension to motivate action. Finding the temporal sweet spot that can keep you motivated without making your Future Self seem too irrelevant can also be challenging. Timing is everything for this perspective taking exercise to work at its best.

The trick to optimizing this strategy is to think about how your task fits in to the framework of your larger goals so that you can identify the best Future Self to converse with. Say, for example, that you are having trouble getting started with your new healthy lifestyle plan of having more vegetarian meals and exercising more regularly because you are worried that you won't enjoy cutting back on meat and are concerned that exercising regularly will be too difficult given your busy schedule. Thus, you are considering procrastinating. The 1-week time frame between your Present and Future Self might be too short to harness the effects of this strategy.

You might instead step back and think about your larger plans to get more fit and feel more energized in the next year so you can go on a backpacking trip across Asia and consider how making changes to your eating habits and lifestyle now can help you achieve this. Eating more vegetarian meals and getting into a regular exercise routine becomes a piece of the larger picture you are trying to create for your Future Self. It is this Future Self that you would write a profile for and write the letter to. Your Future Self in 1 year, after you have gotten into a healthier state and are about to start your once-in-a-lifetime journey is a Future Self who will be important to you and who will be the most affected by the things you or do, not do, today. Taking the perspective of this Future Self so that you can more empathically consider their welfare can help you find new meaning in your task. Also, as I discussed in Chapter 8, when your task is more meaningful you will be less inclined to procrastinate.

In the "Dear Future Self" exercise that follows, I've outlined some instructions to help you get started in your dialogue. These are based on the ideas we've been exploring and the research you just read about. You can use this exercise to help bridge the temporal gap with your Future Self so that you can embrace their perspective, resist the urge to procrastinate, and take the steps needed to make the world that you imagined for that Future Self a reality.

EXERCISE: Dear Future Self

This evidence-informed exercise is designed to help you feel more connected to your Future Self and thus help you put any tasks or goals you are struggling with in perspective. There are five steps involved, so make sure that you block off a good amount of time and complete all steps to get the most from it.

1. **Which Future Self?** Writing and receiving a letter to your Future Self is one way to feel more connected to your Future Self. Before you start this exercise, it's important that you think about which Future Self you will write to.
   (a) What is a task that you are struggling with currently and are at risk of procrastinating?

   _____

   (b) What is the time frame for this task? _____
   (c) If the time frame is less than a year, how might this task contribute to a larger goal that is important to you and that you expect to reach in a year or more? For example, completing a report for work might be part of your larger goal to be promoted down the road. _____

   _____

(continues)

> ## EXERCISE: Dear Future Self (*Continued*)
>
> 2. **Profiling your Future Self:** While you are thinking about a task or goal that you expect will take at least a year to achieve, imagine what your Future Self will be like at that time. Where do you expect to be living? Where will you be working, and what will be your role? What do you expect your Future Self's health will be like? What will you be like? Create a profile of your Future Self using the these and the other questions below. For best results, try to make it as detailed as possible.
>
> **Your Future Self Profile in _____ [add the relevant time frame]**
>
> Age: _____ Occupation and position: _____
>
> Where do you live (city, type of dwelling, etc.)? _____
>
> _____
>
> What activities do you engage in (hobbies, sports, lifestyle, social life)?
>
> _____
>
> How would you describe your Future Self's personality? _____
>
> _____
>
> 3. **Writing to your Future Self:** With the profile of your Future Self in mind, write a letter to that future version of yourself. You can write about anything you wish. The main thing is to try and start a conversation by writing this letter. Although you can write as little or as much as you like, a one-page letter is a good guide. You might want to ask your Future Self questions about what goals they are working on, what their daily life is like, and other questions that you think are relevant. You may also want to tell your Future Self about how you are doing right now and the successes and challenges in your life.

EXERCISE: Dear Future Self (*Continued*)

4. Responding to your Present Self: Now fast forward to the time of your Future Self. Imagine that you are now that Future Self, and you have received the letter written by your Present Self that you just wrote. Write a reply letter as your Future Self back to your Present Self. You may want to reply to the question that your Present Self wrote, and you may also want to ask your Present Self questions about what their daily life is like. The content of the letter is up to you to decide. For best results, aim to write a reply that is about one page.

5. Reflection: Once you have completed this exercise it can be helpful to reflect on how you feel about the Future Self you wrote to. Do you feel any closer? If so, why? If not, what made it difficult for you to connect? Has writing to your Future Self made you think differently about the task and/or goal you were struggling with? These are some questions to get you started, but again, feel free to add any other reflections that may be relevant to your situation. Writing these down in a journal can also be useful, especially if you wish to try this exercise again at a later date to track anything that might have changed.

TIP: To make this even more realistic, you may want to opt for emailing yourself the letter and then replying by return email.

CHAPTER 10

READY, SET, GO!

By failing to prepare, you are preparing to fail.
—Benjamin Franklin

In this chapter, you will learn

- why being prepared to take action is key for reducing procrastination,
- how to procrastination-proof your environment,
- why motivation follows when you take action, and
- how to check whether you are ready to take action and leave procrastination in the rear-view mirror.

Congratulations! You've made it to the final chapter of this book. Now, I say this not because I believe that this book was unpleasant to read (I sincerely hope it wasn't!) or to make some ironic jest about procrastinating reading a book about procrastination. I say it because we have covered a lot of territory on our journey toward understanding procrastination and how to resolve it. Delving into the psychological processes involved in procrastination likely meant that at times it has been difficult for some of you to face up to certain truths about yourself and your habits that you may have preferred to avoid. You may have even had to step away from this book at times to digest what we've covered if it gave you glimpses of aspects of yourself that you'd rather not grapple with. If you did have to take a pause, I hope you were accepting and compassionate toward yourself for doing so. After all, you are here now, ready to explore a few remaining strategies that can help you get closer to having a life in which procrastination is a rare rather than regular occurrence. That's what really matters.

Throughout this book we've viewed procrastination through the lens of mood regulation. We've explored how emotions and difficulties managing negative emotions create the conditions for procrastination. We've examined the source of these emotions, and specifically how our thoughts and beliefs about ourselves (both now and in the future), and the task, play a critical role in understanding procrastination. Drawing on the latest psychological scientific evidence, I've highlighted specific strategies to help you short-circuit the mental and emotional habits and biases that can fuel procrastination and offered a variety of new approaches to managing negative mood so that you won't have to resort to procrastination.

Being armed with the best of intentions, and a good repertoire of approaches for managing your emotions, can get you off to a great start for combating procrastination. Sometimes your efforts will yield exactly what you had hoped for. Other times they will come in at the other end of the spectrum as you find yourself still struggling to get on with that task you know you should be doing. Learning to calibrate which techniques to implement, and when, is also important.

You'll recall that, from the outset, I noted that there's no one-size-fits-all approach to reducing procrastination. If there were, there would be no need for this book. You have to consider that what might work for you may not work for someone else, and what might work for you in one situation, or for one task, may not work in another situation or for a different task. For reasons we discuss shortly, the context in which you work on your tasks can and does make a difference when it comes to implementing approaches to reducing procrastination.

To successfully reduce procrastination, you need to be strategic and develop sustainable habits. This includes setting up the circumstances that will support the techniques and approaches you use to reduce any urges to procrastinate so you can optimize their effectiveness. Even the best toolkit of tips and techniques for tackling procrastination can produce less-than-desirable results if the contexts and conditions that they are applied in create the very difficulties that they are trying to reduce. In short, planning how you will engage with your task, and preparing your environment so that it supports, rather than thwarts, your actions to get your task done, are crucial to ward off any urges to procrastinate.

In this chapter, I outline a three-step strategy that can help you set up the internal and external contexts that will support your momentum as you take action to complete important tasks. I refer to this as the *ready, set, go* approach. Each step in this approach includes evidence-informed insights that can quell negative emotions elicited by internal and external contexts to help you resist getting stuck in the emotional quagmire that feeds procrastination.

READY! THE ART OF BEING PREPARED TO ACT

When it comes to successfully completing a task, the popular Scout motto "Be prepared" is good advice. Launching yourself into a task without knowing what will be involved in its completion can be a quick route to disaster and procrastination. This is often why we procrastinate tasks that are unfamiliar, ambiguous, or with which we have little experience. As research has shown, the uncertainty associated with such tasks is uncomfortable and can sabotage our confidence in how ready we are to proceed (e.g., A. J. Lim & Javadpour, 2021). In contrast, tasks that are well defined and structured tend be those that we view as less aversive and therefore tend to be procrastinated less.

Define the Task

In a perfect world, all of our tasks would be clearly defined, well structured, and leave little to the imagination in terms of how to best execute them. In such a world, procrastination would be less of an issue because people would have a clearer idea of how to prepare for engaging with their tasks. In the real world, though, we often face tasks that are not so well defined or that lack critical details or information. Jumping into such tasks without being fully prepared can cause you to quickly stall on the journey to completing them.

Now, this may just seem like common sense. You wouldn't start a healthy lifestyle plan, for example, if you didn't know what the healthiest foods for you to eat were, how much weekly physical activity is recommended, or the best type of exercise for your age and personal circumstances. For many tasks, these types of parameters can be quite clear to us at the onset. For example, public health messages reinforce the idea that eating fruits and vegetables is healthy and that minimizing the time spent being sedentary is beneficial. But often buried within these seemingly clear directives lie hidden aspects of the task that are much more ambiguous, especially if it's something that is new to us. We know from the research on procrastination that tasks that raise feelings of uncertainty, perhaps because we have insufficient information, can create stress and anxiety, and in turn result in procrastination. In short, task uncertainty is a precursor to procrastination.

One way to prepare, so that your efforts aren't derailed by unexpected uncertainty, is to audit the task before you start. In other words, take stock of whether you have all the necessary information to begin, and what other resources or support you may need to be successful. If you find that you are missing key information or resources, then take steps to fill in these gaps. For example, get in touch with people who have experience with your task, and ask their advice. If details are missing, talk to the person whom you agreed to do the task for to get clarification. This preparation is all about doing what you can to reduce uncertainty you have before you begin.

Although it's true that we don't always know what we don't know, taking steps to audit the task will go a long way toward reducing uncertainty and any urges to procrastinate that this can feed. But it's also easy to get stuck in a holding pattern of overpreparation, if we go too far in our attempts to remove all uncertainty about the task. The goal is to not reduce *all* uncertainty about the task but just enough so that it is more manageable. Being aware of, and managing, any tendencies you might have to overprepare in an attempt to gain a sense of control is crucial for not getting stuck in endless preparation and procrastination.

Taking concrete steps to reduce task-related uncertainty is important for another reason as well. Sometimes we can let our doubts about the task spiral into doubts about our own capabilities for completing the task. But "task doubt" is not the same as self-doubt. Although they may initially feel the same, it's important to distinguish between them and get doubts about the task under control. This especially true if self-doubt is something you struggle with. If you're struggling to make sense out of a task, you likely are missing information or experience. This isn't the same as not being capable enough to complete the task.

Break Large Tasks Into Subtasks to Reduce Stress

Our confidence about whether we can execute a certain task can also be shaken if we view the task a something that is large and complicated. Consider, for example, writing an essay or a report. For a number of reasons, many students find writing an end-of-term essay a daunting task. It often involves reading background material, structuring an outline, following referencing conventions, and then, of course, the writing. When we consider this task as a whole, it can feel overwhelming and be hard to know where to start, and when we feel overwhelmed, we feel stressed. And when we feel stressed about a task, the inclination is to avoid it and procrastinate, as illustrated in the following example:

> Handed an essay in late because I left it to the last minute. I couldn't bring myself to start it as it seemed like such a big and difficult task, so I ignored it until it was almost too late.

Fortunately, there's a trick to resolving the feeling that one is overwhelmed and the action paralysis that often follows. It involves a simple yet elegant strategy that is often used for effective task management: You break that big, overwhelming task down into its component pieces. Now, instead of one complex, large task you are dealing with a series of smaller and more manageable subtasks. So, for example, when faced with writing an essay, you might see this as first doing background reading, followed by setting up an outline, then writing the introduction, and the main points, then the conclusion. When you view the larger task as comprising smaller components, and then think about each one separately, you will feel less threatened. You reduce how aversive it seems, and this helps diminish any self-doubts or fears about failing you may have. This can make it easier to get started working on the task.

Breaking a larger, more complex task down into its components offers some other important advantages. After you take action on and complete the first subtask—for example, doing background reading for your essay or report—you gain a sense of accomplishment and confidence that you actually *can* complete the task. The success from completing this initial subtask builds your confidence in your abilities, or your *self-efficacy*, as it is referred to by psychological scientists (Bandura, 1986).

Decades of research have demonstrated that successful experiences with a task tend to grow our feelings of competence and self-efficacy. This means that each small success we have with the subtasks results in increased confidence that we can complete the next subtask. The more self-efficacy we have, the more likely we will be to persist when we experience unexpected ups and downs on the journey toward our goal. Preparing your task as a series of smaller subtasks rather than one larger, more complex task establishes a momentum of success that can carry you through to complete the overall task.

It's worth mentioning here that we can erode our feelings of self-efficacy if we don't prepare our tasks in the best way. Just as successes build self-efficacy, failures tear it down and breed self-doubt. This is why it is critical to take steps to prepare before starting a task. Making sure you are clear about what is required to complete the task, along with mentally reframing the task as a set of smaller more manageable subtasks, are two key strategies that help you resist procrastinating.

Take a Moment

Think about the last time you successfully completed a task. Ask yourself: "How did I feel afterward?" "Did I find that my confidence and motivation to take on other tasks was strengthened?" "Did I feel empowered?"

SET! SET UP YOUR ENVIRONMENT

Now that you are equipped with your toolkit of strategies to manage your mood and have prepared your tasks so that they are clear and structured into more manageable subtasks, what's next? It would be tempting to simply start writing that report, begin your diet, or launch that home renovation project and hope for the best. If you did, though, you would be overlooking an important element that can factor into whether or not you would be successful, namely, your environment.

Our environment is often the last thing we think about when we are trying to control our procrastination and make progress on our goals and tasks. You might consider your environment in terms of the distractions it holds and think that being aware of them will somehow make you immune to their pull, but unfortunately this is often not the case. The fact is, when it comes to your environment, it's important not to underestimate how challenging it can be for you to overcome the power of a strong situation, especially if you are prone to procrastination.

There are a number of ways your environment can derail your best intentions and lead you down a path to procrastination. Environments that provide an abundance of more pleasurable alternatives to the task on which you are working, or that do not remind you of the reasons why you are working on this task, are those in which it is most challenging to be productive. Such contexts, whether at work or home, make it difficult to follow through with your intentions to get your task done and instead provide a breeding ground for procrastination. I refer to such environments as being *procrastinogenic*.

Editing the Procrastinogenic Environment

Procrastinogenic environments include tempting options that provide a quick fix for mood regulation when you are struggling with a task. From video game consoles, to television, to social media channels and other digital distractions, if your environment includes any reminders of what you could be doing that will make you feel better than working on that newsletter for your community group, it will be that much more difficult to stay on task. And they don't always need to be fun things, either.

It's quite common to swap out that important task that you should be doing for another less urgent or important task. When we work on the smaller tasks, we can fool ourselves into believing that we are being productive. This was when the following individual got caught up with the distraction of small tasks:

> Instead of tackling a single complicated piece of work that would require my concentration and effort for the rest of the day, I allowed myself to be distracted by several smaller, less important tasks. I deluded myself that I was achieving more by achieving all these small unimportant things rather than tackling a single, complex one. I also allowed myself "rewards" after each small task (e.g., checking personal email or social media), but these things also distracted me from getting the important work done.

In this example, the so-called rewards for completing small, less important tasks actually served as another layer of distraction that resulted in further procrastination.

So, how do you manage these procrastination-fostering distractions in your environment? Well, as the old saying goes, out of sight is really out of mind. Setting up your environment to quarantine these distractions so they can't intrude into your mental space while you are working is critical. Putting your smartphone on do-not-disturb mode—or, better still, putting it in another room—and closing browser tabs with your social media channels or email are easy ways to help manage digital distractions.

But it's also important to consider other aspects of your environment that might tempt you to take a longer-than-intended break when you hit a difficult spot in your work. If you're musically inclined, it could mean removing that guitar in the corner from the room. If baking is your go-to, feel-good activity, then be sure that you are not working in an area where the kitchen is in sight. And if meticulous organizing is what gives you pleasure, then by all means make sure you work on your task in an area that is free from disorganization—otherwise, you could find yourself obsessively alphabetizing your spice rack or designing a new filing system for your mp3s instead of making progress with that newsletter.

When you are in a procrastinogenic environment, your surroundings are in effect calling the shots. You may think that you are the one deciding to take a break, but in reality it's the cues around you that are having a subtle but powerful influence on your choices, often pulling you in the direction of procrastination.

Why are these distractions and temptations hard to resist, and why do they override your best intentions to stay on task? From the perspective of psychological science, the answer lies in the temporal dilemma that underlies procrastination: You have to choose between satisfying a short-term, immediate goal to manage your mood and achieving your long-term goal. If you choose to satisfy your immediate goal of short-term mood repair by looking at social media, then you are sacrificing time spent toward writing that newsletter, whose deadline is looming. If you continue to work on the newsletter, which is triggering your self-doubts and fears that you will disappoint others rather than opting for the quick fix of a digital distraction, then you will have to struggle with a negative mood. You have a conflict between two incompatible goals. But because it's difficult to give equal attention to both goals, we often let one or both fade into the background. Whether or not these goals are prominent in your thinking can determine how you choose to resolve this conflict.

This is where cues in your environment can make the difference between which goal you choose. Video game consoles, your smartphone, baking supplies, a guitar, or an organizational task that you have been itching to do can serve as cues that there is something more pleasurable that you could be doing other than calling your friend to have that difficult conversation, or fixing the tiles in the bathroom, or writing that newsletter. These cues remind you of your goal to repair your mood when you are struggling with your task. In psychological terms, this is called *priming*. The cues from your environment prime your goal of short-term mood repair, bringing it to the forefront of your thinking. In essence, your environment has resolved your temporal dilemma by focusing your attention on your short-term goal of repairing your mood and made it harder to think about your long-term goal of completing your report on time or adopting a healthier lifestyle. Because it's easier to think about your short-term goal in this context, you default to that goal and procrastinate your long-term goal.

Research on food cues and people's eating habits is a good example of how powerfully these cues can factor into our decision making and derail our best intentions. Numerous studies have demonstrated that when people are exposed to cues that remind them of tastier but less healthy food options, it is easier for them to break their diets (e.g., Papies, 2012). The cues activate their goal to eat something pleasurable (a short-term goal) and make it harder to think about wanting to eat healthier (a long-term goal). Some individuals, such as those who tend to restrain what they eat, are especially susceptible to these cues and are at greater risk for their goal-derailing effects.

We can think about procrastination in similar terms. If you are prone to procrastination, the cues in your environment will have that much more of a pull on how you resolve your temporal dilemma to feel good (or at least less bad) now, versus making progress on your important task. This is why editing your environment for potential cues that could prime your mood-regulation goals is so crucial before you begin your task. By identifying and removing such cues, you are one step closer to ensuring that your efforts to stay on track and resist procrastination will be fruitful.

You can also capitalize on the power of the cues in your environment to support your efforts to reduce procrastination. Using these same psychological principles, you can seed your surroundings with cues that will prime your long-term goals and their meaningfulness to you. So, for example, if you are working on writing a stellar report, make sure that you keep your notebook and favorite pen, or your tablet or laptop, in plain view, set up and ready to use. Adding encouraging notes in your writing area, such as "You've got this!", can also help. If you are trying to adopt a healthier lifestyle, post pictures of healthy snacks near the kitchen, and place health magazines and pictures of people engaging in your preferred exercise in areas where you might normally be tempted to be more sedentary. People also tend to pay more attention to things that are unexpected or that stand out in the environment; this is called the *salience bias*. You can take advantage of this salience bias by being creative and using images and cues to prime your tasks and goals in unexpected ways. By doing so, you can transform your environment from being one that is procrastinogenic to one that is supportive of task completion.

Take a Moment

Stop for a moment and take a look around your environment. Ask yourself: "Does it promote calm concentration, or is there a lot of 'eye candy' that can distract me if I am trying to focus?" "What elements of my environment might I want to change to make it easier to feel less distracted when I'm working on my important tasks?" "Are there things I can add to my environment to remind me of the goals I am working on and their meaning to me?"

Managing the Trap of Social Distractions

Distractions and temptations that can steer you toward procrastination can also come in other forms that can be a bit more challenging to control. I am referring to distractions from other people. Well-meaning invitations from friends and family to take a break from writing your newsletter to have a chat, to cheat on your diet by ordering pizza, or to binge-watch the latest series on Netflix rather than going for your scheduled run can easily derail you from making progress on your tasks and goals.

As social creatures, we tend to find interactions with the important people in our lives a source of enjoyment, especially if those interactions are linked to an enjoyable activity. But these social distractions also remind us that we could be doing something more interesting, enjoyable, or fun than the task we are struggling with. They offer an immediate opportunity to shift our mood to a more pleasant state and avoid any negative task-related feelings we are experiencing.

Part of the problem is that you never know when these social distractions will appear. Unlike the more controllable cues within our physical and digital environments, social distractions are unpredictable. You are more likely to be caught off guard when these social temptations appear, and thus you will be less likely to resist them.

But just because social distractions can be unpredictable doesn't mean that their impact on your goals can't be controlled. In fact, there is an ingenious science-supported solution for dealing with just these sorts of tempting situations that has been proven to help people resist procrastinating and follow through with their intentions. It involves actually expecting that there can and will be temptations and distractions in your environment that could pull you away from your tasks and derail your best intentions. Once you accept that such interruptions will likely occur, you can take steps to plan how you will respond to them when they inevitably appear and tempt you into procrastinating.

So, how do you plan to be distracted without actually getting distracted? You do this by forming an if–then plan that details exactly what you will say and do when you encounter an anticipated distraction. For example, if you expect that your mother might call during an afternoon that you have blocked off for doing those pesky home repairs, then you plan how you will respond when she does. You might plan to say, "I'd love to chat with you but can't right now as I'm working. Can we catch up at another time?" Or if you expect that your friends will text and invite you out to a party on a night when you have planned to work on your kitchen DIY projects, then you might plan to reply with "Thanks for thinking of me. Unfortunately, I have other plans tonight. I'll meet up with you another time."

The formal term for these if–then plans is *implementation intentions* (Gollwitzer, 1999). They quite literally specify how you are going to follow through with your intentions to stay on track with your task. When you form an implementation intention, you make yourself more aware of the potential social distractions that might derail your best-laid plans. More important, though, by rehearsing a response to these inevitable interruptions you increase the chances that your default response of giving in to these diversions will be overridden by this new response. In effect, you are learning a new way of responding to temptations that sets you up to deal with them in a way that supports taking action instead of procrastinating.

GO! TAKE ACTION

We've now arrived at the third and final strategy that can help you make the most of your procrastination-busting toolkit. Unlike the first two strategies, which involved doing things to prepare your task and set up your environment, this strategy is surprisingly simple: Just go! Take action and start your task. Despite the directness of this strategy, though, it can be difficult for many of us to just start working on a task that we know we should be doing, for a number of reasons that we have discussed throughout this book. That is the essence of procrastination, after all—voluntarily and unnecessarily delaying the start or completion of an intended and important task.

So, why don't we simply act and get started? Once we start a task, we set things in motion. We are on the path to making the goal real instead of keeping it in the safe realm of possibilities. When the goal is just an idea, we can indulge in wishful thinking about how smoothly everything will go on the journey toward reaching it. We don't have to deal with the inevitable emotional ups and downs or possible failures and setbacks that we might experience if we were actually to get started and take action. Wanting to avoid failure and making mistakes can often be enough to keep a person from ever getting started, as illustrated in this statement from someone who struggles with procrastination:

> Tasks that can't be completed RIGHT NOW often feel impossible to me even though I know that once I can just START, I can get things done. In my brain, starting things is the first step toward getting it wrong.

The perfectionistic desire to avoid making mistakes or having a subpar performance can also drive our rationalization that it's okay to delay because our Future Self will do a better job than what we can today. As we discussed in Chapter 9, though, it's often hard to think about the future in concrete, realistic terms. Most times, our Future Self is no more familiar to us than a stranger.

Considering this, it's easy to understand why we might be tempted to not simply get started with our task. If you believe that your Future Self will be much more capable than you are to flawlessly execute your task, then why would you make the effort to start now? In this mythical world of the future your Future Self will be much better able to manage all the difficulties and negative emotions that you can't bring yourself to face today.

Are you struggling with writing that report your manager wants on her desk by the end of the week? No problem—Future You will have all the right ideas and the most convincing ways of presenting the facts to produce a stellar report, so you don't need to work on it today. Feeling tempted to go off your diet and indulge in that oh-so-delicious but calorie-laden piece of chocolate cake instead of the apple that you told yourself you would have as a snack? No worries at all. Go ahead and enjoy it, even if this means you'll probably want seconds. Future You will be brimming with self-control and able to make all the right food choices and resist all such delicious temptations. The problem is that if the future feels abstract and distant, then we are likely to overestimate just how much we will actually change over time. Future You is probably going to be more like Present You than you'd like to admit and have just as much difficulty with your tasks and thus be just as prone to procrastination on that task as you are now.

We might also convince ourselves that tomorrow, but not now, is the perfect time to start our task, and we then procrastinate on those grounds. This is an easy rationalization to make. If we are feeling uncertain, tired, anxious, or stressed, or are simply not in the mood, then why not wait until we feel more motivated? After all, we need to feel motivated to act, right? This type of practical reasoning feeds our tendency to act only when we can explain, and then justify, our actions. It's a common human tendency that philosophers Plato and Aristotle were keen to point out. Getting started on that task when we have more reasons to not act than to act can seem irrational—but remember, so is procrastination.

This is why it's important to strike a balance between (a) preparing the ground so that any anticipated obstacles, distractions, and internal resistances don't stall your momentum once you start and (b) overthinking what you actually need to get started. Surprisingly, motivation is not one of the factors that is essential for getting started. We often believe that we need to be motivated to get started on a task that is making us doubt our competence or that is causing anxiety. But, as William James once said, "Belief creates the actual fact." If we believe we need to feel motivated to get started, then we've made this our reality. We've set up a potential catch-22 situation in which we will delay starting until we are in that perfect state of motivation, where all of our inner and outer forces align in perfect harmony to support that magical moment where we can finally act on our intentions.

However, just as perfection is an illusion, so too is the idea that there is a perfect time to start that task. We often buy into the idea of perfect timing because our reflections on the historical account of events that unfolded when we pursued our previous goals are selective and biased. People have a strong need to make sense out of their world and their experiences and to see the world as being predictable rather than chaotic. So, when we review past events, we tend to selectively recall those that confirm what we know to already be true as a way of making sense from them. For example, if we successfully completed a task or reached a goal, then we must have started at the right time when all the circumstances aligned in our favor. As numerous studies have shown, this *hindsight bias* can lead us to conclude that events are more predictable than what they actually are. This tells us that, in addition to not being very good at predicting our future emotional states when we have to work on a difficult task, we are also lacking when we try to predict when we will feel motivated to start our task.

If we let our hindsight bias operate unchecked, we can idealize these reconstructed moments as exemplars of why waiting for the perfect time to start a task we are putting off is so important. But this is just another post hoc rationalization that fuels procrastination (like believing that we do our best work at the last minute). But who's to say that right now isn't that "perfect" moment to take action? How do you know that by taking action right now to start your task you will be taking advantage of a perfect alignment of forces, circumstances, and your own mood and motivation levels that will lead to the best possible results? Well, actually you don't know, and, unless you have a time machine, you can't know. It could be 30 minutes from now, or 2 days from now, or even a week from now. The truth of the matter is that we simply don't know when it will be *that* perfect time to start the task. Why? Because there is no such thing as the perfect time. Perfect timing is a retrospective concept. It's up to us to decide what the right time is to start.

If your resistance to starting a task now is about motivation, consider this: Motivation comes from taking action. When we simply just get started, we set in motion the very circumstances that will give us the motivation and momentum that we convinced ourselves that we needed to start the task in the first place. Taking action generates the positive emotions and motivation to continue. Recall our discussion of self-efficacy and how small successes grow confidence in our abilities. Just by starting a task you have achieved a milestone—you are no longer procrastinating; you are on your way to completing the task. As an added bonus, you now have experiential proof that you are someone who *can* take action rather than procrastinate. This alone can help you see yourself as someone who can get their tasks done so that you can shed that "procrastinator" label and all the feelings of guilt and shame that come with it.

You can always convince yourself that there will be a better time, a better set of circumstances, and a better state of mind and mood for you act. In doing so, though, you dismiss the opportunities that taking action now presents you to build confidence, quell self-doubt, and find meaning and satisfaction by embarking on the journey of engaging with your tasks and goals. You need instead to recognize that simply getting started with your task will solve most of the problems that you think are keeping you from getting started.

Accept that now, not later, is the right time to take action and start your task. Completing the "Ready, Set, Go" exercise will help you with this.

As the Chinese philosopher Lao Tzu once said, "The journey of a thousand miles begins with one step." Whether yours is a small task or an important goal, now is the best time to take that one step.

EXERCISE: Ready, Set, Go Checklist

1. **Ready?**
   A. Do you have all the information you need to get started with your task?

   ☐ YES ☐ NO

   If not, a bit of research or talking with those who are familiar with your task may be in order before you start to reduce any ambiguities or uncertainties about the task.

   B. Is your task or goal one that consists of a lot of complexities or moving parts?

   ☐ YES ☐ NO

   If yes, then a good strategy before you start is to break it down into smaller, discrete subtasks that can be easily accomplished over a short period of time. Aim for components that make sense as stand-alone tasks and that are not so small that you won't feel any satisfaction from accomplishing them.

2. **Set!**
   A. Are there distractions or other temptations in the immediate environment where you plan to work on your task? Don't forget that digital distractions also matter.

   ☐ YES ☐ NO

(*continues*)

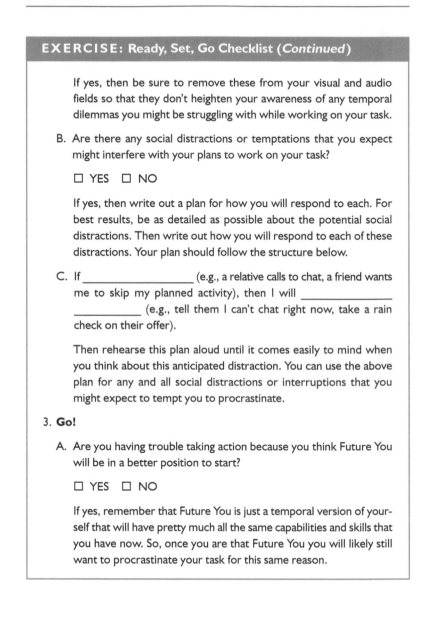

EXERCISE: Ready, Set, Go Checklist (*Continued*)

If yes, then be sure to remove these from your visual and audio fields so that they don't heighten your awareness of any temporal dilemmas you might be struggling with while working on your task.

B. Are there any social distractions or temptations that you expect might interfere with your plans to work on your task?

☐ YES ☐ NO

If yes, then write out a plan for how you will respond to each. For best results, be as detailed as possible about the potential social distractions. Then write out how you will respond to each of these distractions. Your plan should follow the structure below.

C. If _____ (e.g., a relative calls to chat, a friend wants me to skip my planned activity), then I will _____ _____ (e.g., tell them I can't chat right now, take a rain check on their offer).

Then rehearse this plan aloud until it comes easily to mind when you think about this anticipated distraction. You can use the above plan for any and all social distractions or interruptions that you might expect to tempt you to procrastinate.

3. **Go!**

A. Are you having trouble taking action because you think Future You will be in a better position to start?

☐ YES ☐ NO

If yes, remember that Future You is just a temporal version of yourself that will have pretty much all the same capabilities and skills that you have now. So, once you are that Future You you will likely still want to procrastinate your task for this same reason.

EXERCISE: Ready, Set, Go Checklist (*Continued*)

B. Are you waiting for the perfect time to start?

□ YES   □ NO

If yes, remember that a bit of preparation can be good, but too much may be just another way to avoid the task because you are afraid of failure or of not having everything go smoothly. There is no perfect time to start, only the right time, which is now if you are prepared and have set up your environment to support your efforts to complete the task and not procrastinate.

C. Are you having trouble starting because you're not in the right mood or head space or because you don't feel motivated?

□ YES   □ NO

If yes, then remember that taking action will actually create the motivation and mood that you think you need to get started. By taking action, you will have evidence that you can get the task done, and this can motivate you to keep going. This is a situation where putting the cart before the horse actually does work.

D. Are there any other reasons why you haven't started your task yet?

□ YES   □ NO

If yes, then try reviewing some of the other strategies we've discussed throughout this book to see if they may be relevant for your particular situation. Remember that this applies only to tasks that you are unnecessarily and voluntarily delaying. If you've got good reasons to delay, then it isn't technically procrastination.

REFERENCES

Ayton, P., Pott, A., & Elwakili, N. (2007). Affective forecasting: Why can't people predict their emotions? *Thinking & Reasoning, 13*(1), 62–80. https://doi.org/10.1080/13546780600872726

Baird, H. M., Webb, T. L., Sirois, F. M., & Gibson-Miller, J. (2021). Understanding the effects of time perspective: A meta-analysis testing a self-regulatory framework. *Psychological Bulletin, 147*(3), 233–267. https://doi.org/10.1037/bul0000313

Bandura, A. (1986). The explanatory and predictive scope of self-efficacy theory. *Journal of Social and Clinical Psychology, 4*(3), 359–373. https://doi.org/10.1521/jscp.1986.4.3.359

Biskas, M., Sirois, F. M., & Webb, T. L. (2022). *Using social cognition models to understand why people, such as perfectionists, struggle to respond with self-compassion.* [Manuscript submitted for publication]. Department of Psychology, University of Sheffield.

Blouin-Hudon, E.-M. C., & Pychyl, T. A. (2017). A mental imagery intervention to increase future self-continuity and reduce procrastination. *Applied Psychology, 66*(2), 326–352. https://doi.org/10.1111/apps.12088

Blunt, A., & Pychyl, T. A. (1998). Volitional action and inaction in the lives of undergraduate students: State orientation, procrastination and proneness to boredom. *Personality and Individual Differences, 24*(6), 837–846. https://doi.org/10.1016/S0191-8869(98)00018-X

Blunt, A., & Pychyl, T. A. (2000). Task aversiveness and procrastination: A multi-dimensional approach to task aversiveness across stages of personal projects. *Personality and Individual Differences*, 24(6), 837–846. https://doi.org/10.1016/S0191-8869(98)00018-X

Bratman, G. N., Hamilton, J. P., Hahn, K. S., Daily, G. C., & Gross, J. J. (2015). Nature experience reduces rumination and subgenual prefrontal cortex activation. *Proceedings of the National Academy of Sciences of the United States of America*, 112(28), 8567–8572. https://doi.org/10.1073/pnas.1510459112

Breines, J. G., & Chen, S. (2012). Self-compassion increases self-improvement motivation. *Personality and Social Psychology Bulletin*, 38(9), 1133–1143. https://doi.org/10.1177/0146167212445599

Brown, J. D., & Dutton, K. A. (1995). The thrill of victory, the complexity of defeat: Self-esteem and people's emotional reactions to success and failure. *Journal of Personality and Social Psychology*, 68(4), 712–722. https://doi.org/10.1037/0022-3514.68.4.712

Buehler, R., & McFarland, C. (2001). Intensity bias in affective forecasting: The role of temporal focus. *Personality and Social Psychology Bulletin*, 27(11), 1480–1493. https://doi.org/10.1177/01461672012711009

Chishima, Y., & Wilson, A. E. (2020). Conversation with a future self: A letter-exchange exercise enhances student self-continuity, career planning, and academic thinking. *Self and Identity*. Advance online publication. https://doi.org/10.1080/15298868.2020.1754283

Chowdhury, S. F., & Pychyl, T. A. (2018). A critique of the construct validity of active procrastination. *Personality and Individual Differences*, 120, 7–12. https://doi.org/10.1016/j.paid.2017.08.016

Chu, A. H. C., & Choi, J. N. (2005). Rethinking procrastination: Positive effects of "active" procrastination behavior on attitudes and performance. *The Journal of Social Psychology*, 145(3), 245–264. https://doi.org/10.3200/SOCP.145.3.245-264

Daily Mail. (2013, September 16). Diet starts today. . . and ends on Friday: How we quickly slip back into bad eating habits within a few days. https://www.dailymail.co.uk/news/article-2421737/Diet-starts-today—ends-Friday-How-quickly-slip-bad-eating-habits-days.html

Davies, T. (2017, August 17). Survey reveals how much time we really waste in the working day. *Reboot Online*. https://www.rebootonline.com/blog/survey-reveals-how-much-time-we-really-waste-in-the-working-day/

Ersner-Hershfield, H., Wimmer, G. E., & Knutson, B. (2009). Saving for the future self: Neural measures of future self-continuity predict temporal discounting. *Social Cognitive and Affective Neuroscience, 4*(1), 85–92. https://doi.org/10.1093/scan/nsn042

Ewert, C., Vater, A., & Schröder-Abé, M. (2021). Self-compassion and coping: A meta-analysis. *Mindfulness, 12,* 1063–1077. https://doi.org/10.1007/s12671-020-01563-8

Flett, G. L., Blankstein, K. R., & Martin, T. R. (1995). Procrastination, negative self-evaluation, and stress in depression and anxiety: A review and preliminary model. In J. R. Ferrari, J. H. Johnson, & W. G. McCown (Eds.), *Procrastination and task avoidance: Theory, research, and treatment* (pp. 137–167). Plenum.

Flett, G. L., Stainton, M., Hewitt, P., Sherry, S., & Lay, C. (2012). Procrastination automatic thoughts as a personality construct: An analysis of the procrastinatory cognitions inventory. *Journal of Rational-Emotive & Cognitive-Behavior Therapy, 30*(4), 223–236. https://doi.org/10.1007/s10942-012-0150-z

Gilbert, D. T., Pinel, E. C., Wilson, T. D., Blumberg, S. J., & Wheatley, T. P. (1998). Immune neglect: A source of durability bias in affective forecasting. *Journal of Personality and Social Psychology, 75*(3), 617–638. https://doi.org/10.1037/0022-3514.75.3.617

Gilbert, P. (2009). Introducing compassion-focused therapy. *Advances in Psychiatric Treatment, 15*(3), 199–208. https://doi.org/10.1192/apt.bp.107.005264

Gilbert, P., & Procter, S. (2006). Compassionate mind training for people with high shame and self-criticism: Overview and pilot study of a group therapy approach. *Clinical Psychology and Psychotherapy, 13,* 353–379. https://www.doi.org/10.1002/cpp.507

Gollwitzer, P. M. (1999). Implementation intentions: Strong effects of simple plans. *American Psychologist, 54*(7), 493–503. https://doi.org/10.1037/0003-066X.54.7.493

Heintzelman, S. J., & King, L. A. (2014). Life is pretty meaningful. *American Psychologist, 69*(6), 561–574. https://doi.org/10.1037/a0035049

Hen, M., & Goroshit, M. (2018). General and life-domain procrastination in highly educated adults in Israel. *Frontiers in Psychology, 9*(1173), 1173. https://doi.org/10.3389/fpsyg.2018.01173

Hershfield, H. E. (2011). Future self-continuity: How conceptions of the future self transform intertemporal choice. *Annals of the New York Academy of Sciences, 1235*(1), 30–43. https://doi.org/10.1111/j.1749-6632.2011.06201.x

Human Resources Online. (2020). *How much time are your employees spending procrastinating?* https://www.humanresourcesonline.net/how-much-time-are-your-employees-spending-procrastinating

Jiao, Q., Da-Ros Voseles, D. A., Collins, K. M. T., & Onwuegbuzie, A. J. (2011). Academic procrastination and the performance of graduate-level cooperative groups in research methods courses. *Journal of the Scholarship of Teaching and Learning, 11*(1), 119–138.

Kaftan, O. J., & Freund, A. M. (2020). How to work out and avoid procrastination: The role of goal focus. *Journal of Applied Social Psychology, 50*(3), 145–159. https://doi.org/10.1111/jasp.12646

Kelley, W. M., Macrae, C. N., Wyland, C. L., Caglar, S., Inati, S., & Heatherton, T. H. (2002). Finding the self? An event-related fMRI study. *Journal of Cognitive Neuroscience, 14*(5), 785–794. https://doi.org/10.1162/08989290260138672

Kim, K., del Carmen Triana, M., Chung, K., & Oh, N. (2016). When do employees cyberloaf? An interactionist perspective examining personality, justice, and empowerment. *Human Resource Management, 55*(6), 1041–1058. https://doi.org/10.1002/hrm.21699

Kim, K. R., & Seo, E. H. (2015). The relationship between procrastination and academic performance: A meta-analysis. *Personality and Individual Differences, 82*, 26–33. https://doi.org/https://doi.org/10.1016/j.paid.2015.02.038

Kroese, F. M., Evers, C., Adriaanse, M. A., & de Ridder, D. T. (2016). Bedtime procrastination: A self-regulation perspective on sleep insufficiency in the general population. *Journal of Health Psychology, 21*(5), 853–862. https://doi.org/10.1177/1359105314540014

Legood, A., Lee, A., Schwarz, G., & Newman, A. (2018). From self-defeating to other defeating: Examining the effects of leader procrastination on follower work outcomes. *Journal of Occupational and Organizational Psychology, 91*(2), 430–439. https://doi.org/10.1111/joop.12205

Lim, A. J., & Javadpour, S. (2021). Into the unknown: Uncertainty and procrastination in students from a life history perspective. *Frontiers in Psychology, 12*(3541). https://doi.org/10.3389/fpsyg.2021.717380

Lim, V. K. G., & Chen, D. J. (2012). Cyberloafing at the workplace: Gain or drain on work? *Behaviour Information & Technology, 31*(4), 343–353.

Lyubomirsky, S., Sheldon, K. M., & Schkade, D. (2005). Pursuing happiness: The architecture of sustainable change. *Review of General Psychology, 9*(2), 111–131. https://doi.org/10.1037/1089-2680.9.2.111

McCrea, S. M., Liberman, N., Trope, Y., & Sherman, S. J. (2008). Construal level and procrastination. *Psychological Science, 19*(12), 1308–1314. https://doi.org/10.1111/j.1467-9280.2008.02240.x

McLaughlin, K. A., & Nolen-Hoeksema, S. (2011). Rumination as a transdiagnostic factor in depression and anxiety. *Behaviour Research and Therapy, 49*(3), 186–193. https://doi.org/10.1016/j.brat.2010.12.006

Meier, A., Reinecke, L., & Meltzer, C. E. (2016). "Facebocrastination"? Predictors of using Facebook for procrastination and its effects on students' well-being. *Computers in Human Behavior, 64,* 65–76. https://doi.org/10.1016/j.chb.2016.06.011

Metin, U. B., Taris, T. W., & Peeters, M. C. W. (2016). Measuring procrastination at work and its associated workplace aspects. *Personality and Individual Differences, 101,* 254–263. https://doi.org/10.1016/j.paid.2016.06.006

Myrick, J. G. (2015). Emotion regulation, procrastination, and watching cat videos online: Who watches internet cats, why, and to what effect? *Computers in Human Behavior, 52,* 168–176. https://doi.org/10.1016/j.chb.2015.06.001

Neff, K. D. (2011). Self-compassion, self-esteem, and well-being. *Social and Personality Psychology Compass, 5*(1), 1–12. https://doi.org/10.1111/j.1751-9004.2010.00330.x

Papies, E. K. (2012). Goal priming in dieters: Recent insights and applications. *Current Obesity Reports, 1*(2), 99–105. https://doi.org/10.1007/s13679-012-0009-8

Patrzek, J., Sattler, S., van Veen, F., Grunschel, C., & Fries, S. (2015). Investigating the effect of academic procrastination on the frequency and variety of academic misconduct: A panel study. *Studies in Higher Education, 40*(6), 1014–1029. https://doi.org/10.1080/03075079.2013.854765

Phillips, A. G., & Silvia, P. J. (2005). Self-awareness and the emotional consequences of self-discrepancies. *Personality and Social Psychology Bulletin, 31*(5), 703–713. https://doi.org/10.1177/0146167204271559

Pinxten, M., De Laet, T., Van Soom, C., Peeters, C., & Langie, G. (2019). Purposeful delay and academic achievement: A critical review of the

Active Procrastination Scale. *Learning and Individual Differences*, *73*, 42–51. https://doi.org/10.1016/j.lindif.2019.04.010

Reinecke, L., Meier, A., Aufenanger, S., Beutel, M. E., Dreier, M., Quiring, O., Stark, B., Wölfling, K., & Müller, K. W. (2018). Permanently online and permanently procrastinating? The mediating role of internet use for the effects of trait procrastination on psychological health and well-being. *New Media & Society*, *20*(3), 862–880. https://doi.org/10.1177/1461444816675437

Robinson, K. J., Mayer, S., Allen, A. B., Terry, M., Chilton, A., & Leary, M. R. (2016). Resisting self-compassion: Why are some people opposed to being kind to themselves? *Self and Identity*, *15*(5), 505–524. https://doi.org/10.1080/15298868.2016.1160952

Ross, M., & Wilson, A. E. (2003). Autobiographical memory and conceptions of self: Getting better all the time. *Current Directions in Psychological Science*, *12*(2), 66–69. https://doi.org/10.1111/1467-8721.01228

Schmall, T. (2018, June 12). You're not the only one putting off your DIY projects. *The New York Post*. https://nypost.com/2018/06/12/youre-not-the-only-one-putting-off-your-diy-projects/

Shaw, G. (2011, January 19). Brits waste £37m on unused gym memberships. *Which?* https://www.which.co.uk/news/2011/01/brits-waste-37m-on-unused-gym-memberships-242448/

Sirois, F. M. (2014a). Out of sight, out of time? A meta-analytic investigation of procrastination and time perspective. *European Journal of Personality*, *28*(5), 511–520. https://doi.org/10.1002/per.1947

Sirois, F. M. (2014b). Procrastination and stress: Exploring the role of self-compassion. *Self and Identity*, *13*(2), 128–145. https://doi.org/10.1080/15298868.2013.763404

Sirois, F. M. (2015). Is procrastination a vulnerability factor for hypertension and cardiovascular disease? Testing an extension of the procrastination–health model. *Journal of Behavioral Medicine*, *38*(3), 578–589. https://doi.org/10.1007/s10865-015-9629-2

Sirois, F. M. (2016, August 15–19). *Embracing the future self: Self-compassion, future self-continuity, and health behaviours* [Paper presentation]. Third International Conference on Time Perspective, Copenhagen, Denmark.

Sirois, F. M., Bogels, S., & Emerson, L. (2019). Self-compassion improves parental well-being in response to challenging parenting events. *The Journal of Psychology*, *153*(3), 327–341. https://doi.org/10.1080/00223980.2018.1523123

Sirois, F. M., & Giguère, B. (2018). Giving in when feeling less good: Procrastination, action control, and social temptations. *British Journal of Social Psychology, 57*(2), 404–427. https://doi.org/10.1111/bjso.12243

Sirois, F. M., Molnar, D. S., & Hirsch, J. K. (2017). A meta-analytic and conceptual update on the associations between procrastination and multidimensional perfectionism. *European Journal of Personality, 31*(2), 137–159. https://doi.org/10.1002/per.2098

Sirois, F. M., & Pychyl, T. A. (2002, August 22–25). *Academic procrastination: Costs to health and well-being* [Paper presentation]. 110th Annual Convention of the American Psychological Association, Chicago, IL.

Sirois, F. M., & Pychyl, T. (2013). Procrastination and the priority of short term mood regulation: Consequences for future self. *Social and Personality Psychology Compass, 7*(2), 115–127. https://doi.org/10.1111/spc3.12011

Sirois, F. M., Shucard, H., & Hirsch, J. K. (2014, July 29–August 1). *Procrastination and perceptions of the future self: Implications for health and well-being* [Paper presentation]. Out of sight, out of time? New perspectives on procrastination, future orientation, and well-being. Second International Conference on Time Perspective, Warsaw, Poland.

Sirois, F. M., van Eerde, W., & Argiropoulou, M. I. (2015). Is procrastination related to sleep quality? Testing an extension of the procrastination-health model. *Cogent Psychology, 2*(1), Article 1074776. https://doi.org/10.1080/23311908.2015.1074776

Sirois, F. M., & Yang, S. (2021). *Procrastination and social support* [Manuscript in preparation]. Department of Psychology, University of Sheffield.

Sirois, F. M., Yang, S., & van Eerde, W. (2019). Development and validation of the General Procrastination Scale (GPS-9): A short and reliable measure of trait procrastination. *Personality and Individual Differences, 146*, 26–33. https://doi.org/10.1016/j.paid.2019.03.039

Stead, R., Shanahan, M. J., & Neufeld, R. W. J. (2010). "I'll go to therapy, eventually": Procrastination, stress and mental health. *Personality and Individual Differences, 49*(3), 175–180. https://doi.org/10.1016/j.paid.2010.03.028

Steel, P. (2007). The nature of procrastination: A meta-analytic and theoretical review of quintessential self-regulatory failure. *Psychological Bulletin, 133*(1), 65–94. https://doi.org/10.1037/0033-2909.133.1.65

Tice, D. M., & Baumeister, R. F. (1997). Longitudinal study of procrastination, performance, stress, and health: The costs and benefits of dawdling. *Psychological Science*, *8*(6), 454–458. https://doi.org/10.1111/j.1467-9280.1997.tb00460.x

Tice, D. M., Bratslavsky, E., & Baumeister, R. F. (2001). Emotional distress regulation takes precedence over impulse control: If you feel bad, do it! *Journal of Personality and Social Psychology*, *80*(1), 53–67. https://doi.org/10.1037/0022-3514.80.1.53

van Eerde, W., & Klingsieck, K. B. (2018). Overcoming procrastination? A meta-analysis of intervention studies. *Educational Research Review*, *25*, 73–85. https://doi.org/https://doi.org/10.1016/j.edurev.2018.09.002

van Eerde, W., & Sirois, F. M. (2021). *Similarity and compensation: The role of procrastination in co-worker dyads for co-worker exchange and satisfaction.* [Manuscript in preparation]. Amsterdam Business School, University of Amsterdam.

Wohl, M. J. A., DeShea, L., & Wahkinney, R. L. (2008). Looking within: Measuring state self-forgiveness and its relationship to psychological well-being. *Canadian Journal of Behavioural Science*, *40*(1), 1–10. https://doi.org/10.1037/0008-400x.40.1.1.1

Wohl, M. J. A., Pychyl, T. A., & Bennett, S. H. (2010). I forgive myself, now I can study: How self-forgiveness for procrastinating can reduce future procrastination. *Personality and Individual Differences*, *48*(7), 803–808. https://doi.org/10.1016/j.paid.2010.01.029

Yang, S., Sirois, F. M., & von Bastian, C. (2021). *Enhancing goal-related meaning and positive emotions to reduce procrastination* [Manuscript in preparation]. Department of Psychology, University of Sheffield.

INDEX

ABOUT THE AUTHOR

Fuschia M. Sirois, PhD, is a professor in the Department of Psychology at Durham University, Durham, England, and is a former Canada Research Chair in Health and Well-Being. For more than 20 years, she has researched the causes and consequences of procrastination as well as how emotions play a role in procrastination. Her research also examines the role of positive psychology traits, states, and interventions for supporting self-regulation and enhancing health and well-being. Prof. Sirois writes and presents talks for academic audiences and the general public on topics that include gratitude, self-compassion, loneliness, perfectionism, and how procrastination is linked to mood. Follow her on Twitter @FuschiaSirois.